Sentences and Fragments

> **A sentence is a group of words which expresses a complete thought.**
>   We went to the party.
>   Will you go to the party with me?
> **A fragment is a group of words punctuated like a sentence but not expressing a complete thought.**
>   When we left the party.
>   And then the cake.

• Write **S** before each group of words that is a sentence. Write **F** before each group of words that is a fragment.

_____ 1. You should go to the doctor for a physical.

_____ 2. A visit to the dentist makes me nervous.

_____ 3. Shots in the arm.

_____ 4. People in the waiting room.

_____ 5. Always tell the doctor exactly where it hurts.

_____ 6. When the nurse comes in.

_____ 7. Did you have any cavities this time?

_____ 8. The surgery was successful.

_____ 9. If you go to the hospital.

_____ 10. He filled out the medical form incorrectly.

_____ 11. Then the doctor.

_____ 12. Are you feeling better now?

_____ 13. I feel wonderful!

_____ 14. Please make me some more soup.

• Add words either before or after the following fragments to construct complete sentences.

1. When I broke my arm. _____

_____

2. If you go to visit Henry. _____

_____

3. To mend his broken bone. _____

_____

IF8732 Grammar 7–8

Recognizing Sentences

> **A sentence expresses a complete thought. It should begin with a capital letter and end with a period (.), question mark (?), or exclamation point (!).**

- Look at the examples below and underline the sentences. If a group of words is not a sentence, add words to make it a sentence and write the sentence on the line.

1. Portugal is in Europe.

   _____

2. On the same peninsula as Spain.

   _____

3. Both countries occupy the Iberian Peninsula.

   _____

4. Bordered by the Mediterranean Sea and the Atlantic Ocean, with water on three sides.

   _____

5. Portugal is much smaller than Spain.

   _____

6. It has a different language, although Portuguese is similar to Spanish.

   _____

7. Because both languages are based on Latin.

   _____

8. Why do you want to go to Portugal?

   _____

9. To see the beautiful scenery, which is world famous.

   _____

10. Visiting Portugal has always been my dream.

    _____

- In each example below, use the words to make a sentence. Remember that each sentence must express a complete thought, begin with a capital letter, and end with a period, question mark or exclamation point.

1. boy, dog, fast _____

2. shellfish, cooked, rice _____

3. difficult, sentences, long, written _____

   _____

4. where, Spain, asked _____

Simple Subjects and Predicates

> **The simple subject names the person or thing the sentence is about. It does not include articles or modifying words.**
>
> The <u>girl</u> in the red hat ran to the corner.
>
> **The simple predicate tells what the subject is or does. It does not include any modifying words. The simple predicate is a verb or a verb phrase.**
>
> The main city library <u>is expanding</u> its shelves.
>
> John Maynard Keynes <u>was</u> an economist.

- In each of the following sentences, underline the simple subject once and the simple predicate twice.

1. One African bird is named the honey guide.

2. The favorite food of the honey guide is beeswax from the nests of wild bees.

3. The nests are too strong for the honey guide, though.

4. So the clever bird enlists the aid of an ally.

5. The unlikely ally is an animal called the ratel.

6. The black and white ratel is called the "honey badger" by many people.

7. Rich, sweet honey is the ratel's favorite food.

8. The ratel's thick, loose skin resists bee stings.

9. The smart bird finds a bees' nest.

10. It chatters to the ratel.

11. The chattering bird leads the ratel to the nest.

12. The ratel breaks the nest with its strong claws.

13. The hungry animal eats the honey.

14. Then the happy bird eats the wax from the broken nest.

Complete Subjects and Predicates

The complete subject of a sentence tells what the sentence is about. It may be one word or many words.

The boy from Michigan is the world geography champion.

He knew the answer to every question they asked him.

The complete predicate tells what the subject is or does. It may be one word or many words.

He knew the answer to every question they asked him.

The young student won.

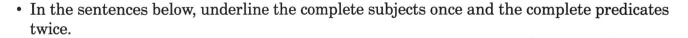

- In the sentences below, underline the complete subjects once and the complete predicates twice.

1. The people in many parts of the world are unable to feed themselves in times of disaster.

2. International relief agencies and many governments try to send aid to those people.

3. The most famous international relief agency is the Red Cross.

4. The Red Cross was founded in 1864 to aid victims of war.

5. Red Cross workers fight misery in times of both war and peace.

6. Over 135 nations have Red Cross societies.

7. Each Red Cross society runs its own program.

8. The American Red Cross has more than 10 million volunteers.

9. Voluntary contributions fund the programs and services of the American Red Cross.

10. All aid to disaster victims is free.

- Write a short paragraph about an organization whose purpose you admire. In each sentence underline the complete subject once and the complete predicate twice.

_____

_____

_____

_____

_____

_____

                                       IF8732 Grammar 7–8

Compound Subjects and Predicates

> **A compound subject contains two or more subjects usually joined by *and* or *or*.**
>   <u>Mark Twain</u> and <u>Harper Lee</u> are American authors.
> **A compound predicate has two or more predicates usually joined by *and, or*, or *but*.**
>   They <u>wrote great novels</u> and <u>became famous</u>.

- In each of the following sentences, turn the subject into a compound subject and write the new sentence on the line. If necessary, change the verb to agree with the compound subject. For instance, "Anne <u>plays</u> softball," but "Anne and Toni <u>play</u> softball."

1. Mary is the best student in math class.

   _____

2. Sycamore trees are my favorite trees.

   _____

3. Birds live in trees.

   _____

4. Light is necessary for a plant to grow.

   _____

5. Anna is my best friend.

   _____

6. Charlie is on the baseball team.

   _____

- In each of the following sentences, turn the predicate into a compound predicate using **and, or,** or **but**. Write the new sentence on the line.

1. Kristy dribbled to the foul line.

   _____

2. Tom painted a picture for the show.

   _____

3. My father lit the barbecue.

   _____

4. Earl bought a new CD.

   _____

Declarative Sentences

> **A declarative sentence makes a statement and ends with a period.**
> The sky is blue.
> The car drove past slowly.
> There are ducks in Central Park.

- For each of these declarative sentences, circle the words that should be capitalized and add punctuation.

1. an avalanche struck the village

2. the snow swept down the mountain

3. many homes were damaged

4. avalanche warnings were given by the Forest Service

5. the people of the village were evacuated in time

6. the avalanche carried rock debris with it onto the highway

7. it was believed to have been started by a car backfiring

8. fortunately not one person was injured

9. there is a lot of avalanche research being done in Switzerland

10. everyone should be aware of the potential dangers of avalanches

11. an avalanche is a mass of snow that slides down a mountain slope

12. most avalanches result from weather conditions

- Write five declarative sentences about a tornado, a hurricane, or a flood.

1. _____

2. _____

3. _____

4. _____

5. _____

Interrogative Sentences

> **An interrogative sentence asks a question and ends with a question mark.**
>   Where is the truck?
>   What time is the game?
>   When will we be going?

- For each of these interrogative sentences, circle the words that should be capitalized and add punctuation.

  1. were you born in Canada

  2. what form of government does Canada have

  3. what is their monetary unit

  4. when did you travel to Canada for your vacation

  5. what languages do Canadians speak

  6. is it a beautiful country

- Change the following declarative sentences into interrogative sentences by changing some of the words, the word order, the capitalization, and the punctuation. For example: "He told me the answer." becomes "Did he tell me the answer?"

  1. I like ice cream.

  _____

  2. We are going to the beach.

  _____

  3. Jake caught 30 fish from the pier.

  _____

  4. Sun block is the most important thing to remember to bring.

  _____

  5. There were no seagulls visible on the beach.

  _____

  6. The waves crashed against the shore.

  _____

  7. The sun glowed on the horizon.

  _____

Imperative Sentences

> **An imperative sentence commands or requests. It ends with a period or an exclamation point. The subject "you" is understood.**
> Don't try it!
> Please walk the dog.
> Fill the collection basket.

- For each of these imperative sentences, circle the word that should be capitalized and add punctuation.

1. find out how this problem should be solved

2. get out of the way

3. please drive defensively

4. clean your room

5. please try to understand my point of view

6. don't walk on the grass

7. please pack me a picnic lunch

8. don't try this at home

9. start the car and let it idle

10. cook the fish and serve it to your friends

- Write five imperative statements that a science teacher might make during a science lab. Be sure to use proper capitalization and punctuation. Do not use quotation marks.

1. _____

2. _____

3. _____

4. _____

5. _____

     IF8732 Grammar 7–8

nd Compound Sentences

ence contains one independent clause.

into the center of town.

histled past.

s in.

entence contains two independent clauses which are closely related.
usually joins the two clauses. Remember to put a comma after the
d before the conjunction that joins the two clauses.

ayed hard, and they won the game easily.

w-scoring game, but it is very exciting.

kicked the ball, and the goalie grabbed it.

sentences (S) and compound sentences (C) by writing an S or C in each blank.
e the simple subjects once and the simple predicates twice.

rtres Cathedral is a masterpiece of Gothic architecture, and it has become a
andmark.

of Chartres is built on the bank of the Eure River.

is located in north-central France, and it is the capital of Eure-et-Loire.

edral has two bell towers.

als of this type were often the focal point of the community, and people
es devoted their entire lives to the construction of these religious buildings.

the year 1194 destroyed most of the cathedral, but it was rebuilt between 1194
.

le sentences and two compound sentences about other famous buildings.

_____

_____

_____

_____

_____

_____

Exclamatory Sentences

> An exclamatory sentence can be either
> a statement or a command made with
> strong feeling. It ends with an
> exclamation point.
>   Hold it right there!
>   Stop!
>   Don't believe it!

- For each of these exclamatory sentences, circle the word that must be capitalized and
  add punctuation.

  1. look at that

  2. this is my favorite food

  3. what a terrific play we saw

  4. it's a home run

  5. my brother passed the exam

  6. grandmother is coming to visit

  7. what a fantastic day that was

  8. we won

  9. what an exquisite painting that is

  10. this is the most amazing thing that has ever happened to me

- Write five exclamatory sentences you might hear at a baseball, basketball, or football game.

  1. _____

  2. _____

  3. _____

  4. _____

  5. _____

Recognizing Kinds of Sentences

> **There are four kinds of sentences: declarative, interrogative, imperative, and exclamatory.**
> **Declarative sentences make a statement and end with a period.**
>   The sky is blue.
> **Interrogative sentences ask a question and end with a question mark.**
>   What color is the sky?
> **Imperative sentences command or request and end with a period or an exclamation point.**
>   Paint the sky blue on your mural.
> **Exclamatory sentences either make a statement or a command with strong feeling and end with an exclamation point.**
>   That's the bluest sky I've ever seen!

• Label the following sentences declarative (**D**), interrogative (**IN**), imperative (**IM**), or exclamatory (**E**).

_____ 1. Clouds are the best free show in the world.

_____ 2. How can you say that?

_____ 3. Just look at them!

_____ 4. They all look the same to me, I'm afraid.

_____ 5. Pay attention while I show you the differences.

_____ 6. Those big, white clouds are cumulus clouds.

_____ 7. Did you know that the ones that look like strands of hair are called cirrus clouds?

_____ 8. Stratus clouds look like they're in layers, or strata.

_____ 9. Nimbus clouds are rain clouds.

_____ 10. They are my favorites!

_____ 11. What kinds of clouds are in the sky today?

_____ 12. Is rain on the way?

_____ 13. The clouds are blocking the sun.

_____ 14. Jets fly right through them!

• Write one of each type of sentence about a trip on a plane.

1. (declarative) _____

2. (interrogative) _____

3. (imperative) _____

4. (exclamatory) _____

Changing Sentences

• Below are 12 answers written as declarative sentences. Writ[e]
in the form of interrogative sentences.
   Example: "The sky is blue." The question might be this: "[W...]

1. My favorite sculptor is Michelangelo.

_____

2. His full name was Michelangelo Buonarroti.

_____

3. He was from Italy.

_____

4. He is also famous for his paintings and architecture.

_____

5. His most famous piece of sculpture is the "Pietà."

_____

6. He also sculpted a famous statue called "David."

_____

7. He lived from 1475 to 1564.

_____

8. He died in the middle of the 16th century.

_____

9. His most famous paintings are on the ceiling of the Sisti[ne]

_____

10. They have recently been restored to their original colors[.]

_____

11. It took several years to complete the restoration.

_____

12. The Sistine Chapel is located in Vatican City.

_____

• Write four types of sentences about another famous artist.

1. (declarative) _____

2. (interrogative) _____

3. (imperative) _____

4. (exclamatory) _____

Simple a[nd]

> **A simple sent[ence]**
>   John walke[d]
>   The train w[...]
>   The doctor i[...]
> **A compound [...]**
> **A conjunctio[n...]**
> **first clause a[nd]**
>   The team p[...]
>   Soccer is a [...]
>   The forwar[d...]

• Identify simple [...]
Then, underlin[e...]

_____ 1. The Cha[...]
        famous [...]

_____ 2. The tow[...]

_____ 3. Chartre[...]

_____ 4. The cat[...]

_____ 5. Cathedr[...]
        sometim[...]

_____ 6. A fire i[n...]
        and 123[...]

• Write two sim[ple...]

1. (simple) __[...]

_____

2. (simple) __[...]

_____

3. (compound [...]

_____

4. (compound [...]

_____

Complex Sentences

> **A complex sentence contains one independent clause and one or more dependent clauses.**
> (The independent clauses are underlined once; the dependent, twice.)
> The fish jumped over the dam when the wave crested.
> If you go to the store, buy me a candy bar.
> The carpenter who built this house is my brother.

- In the following complex sentences, underline the independent clauses once and the dependent clauses twice.

1. The astronauts left the vehicle when the solar panel failed.

2. The United States became serious about space exploration when the Soviet Union launched Sputnik 1.

3. If there is life on the moon, humans have not succeeded in finding it.

4. When a spacecraft is put in orbit, many people share the credit.

5. John Glenn, who was the first American to orbit the earth, became a senator.

6. The Apollo program had a lunar module that was capable of landing on the moon and returning to the main vehicle.

7. The Sputnik 1, which was launched in 1957, was the first artificial satellite.

8. When Neil Armstrong stepped onto the lunar surface, he was fulfilling a promise made by President Kennedy earlier in the decade.

9. The United States launched the space shuttle Columbia, which was the first reusable manned spacecraft.

10. The Challenger, which had seven astronauts on board, exploded in midair.

11. Because this disaster was so devastating, all missions were temporarily stopped.

- Write three complex sentences which tell about space exploration.

1. _____

2. _____

3. _____

Compound/Complex Sentences

> A compound/complex sentence contains two or more independent clauses and at least one dependent clause.
>   The independent clauses are underlined once; the dependent, twice.
>   When the game was over, Seth took the ball, and Larry threw it into the stands.

• In these compound/complex sentences, underline the independent clauses once and the dependent clauses twice.

1. If you have a solution, let us know, and we will try it.

2. Because Trudy had studied previous chess matches, she was able to play brilliantly, and she beat Sid soundly.

3. When we get to the park, Bill will put up the tent, and Carl will start the fire.

4. Though the steak was not fully cooked, Judy cut it, and Ned ate it.

5. Wendell had never gone to college, and he worked at the factory until he won a scholarship.

6. The food was free, and the people who came enjoyed it.

7. Though it was brand new, the stereo would not play, and it destroyed my tape.

8. Because Jenny broke her arm, she could not play in the concert, and the orchestra sounded terrible.

9. Sara suggested the movie, and Elliot and Michael agreed when they heard her choice.

10. Steven went back to Florida, where he opened a law firm, but it was not a financial success.

11. The enraged inventor sued the company, but when he finally won his case, he was deeply in debt.

• In a book or magazine find three examples of compound/complex sentences. Write them here.

1. _____

2. _____

3. _____

Recognizing Sentence Types

A simple sentence contains one independent clause.

A compound sentence contains two independent clauses joined by a conjunction. Remember to put a comma after the first clause and before the conjunction that joins them.

A complex sentence contains one independent clause and one or more dependent clauses.

A compound/complex sentence contains two or more independent clauses and at least one dependent clause.

- Identify the following sentences as Simple **(S)**, Compound **(C)**, Complex **(CX)**, or Compound/ Complex **(C/CX)**.

_____ 1. Whenever a new video game is developed, we immediately go to the store, and my mom looks it over carefully.

_____ 2. The car hit the tree, but there was no damage.

_____ 3. If the camping trip is cancelled, Jake will stay home, but Colleen will probably go to a movie.

_____ 4. When you get to the store, you will be given a free gift.

_____ 5. The teacher, who tried to take charge, was very stern, but the class didn't pay much attention to him.

_____ 6. Kevin tried to get the pump started.

_____ 7. The disc jockey was on the air, and his replacement was waiting in the next room.

_____ 8. A city must be planned carefully, or people will not want to live in it.

_____ 9. We were going to attend the game, but it started raining.

_____ 10. I am going to do my homework after school, but I would rather play with my friends.

_____ 11. Sheila put a dollar into the pop machine, but nothing came out.

_____ 12. The book was exciting and easy to read.

_____ 13. Harry sang the song for his mom, and she loved it.

_____ 14. Because the computer was a very expensive purchase, Dad bought a special table for it, and he kept it in an air-conditioned room.

Fragments

A sentence contains a subject and a verb and expresses a complete thought. A group of words that is punctuated like a sentence but does not contain a complete thought is called a fragment. Often the reason the fragment does not express a complete thought is that it lacks a subject or verb.

Fragments:

Went home past the supermarket.

The reason I missed school yesterday.

Because I wanted.

And her brother.

Sometimes you can correct a fragment by adding a word or words. Other times you can make the correction by connecting the fragment to a sentence and changing the punctuation.

Incorrect: On the way to school, I saw Amy. And her brother.

Correct: On the way to school, I saw Amy and her brother.

• Correct each of the fragments below by adding a word or words to make a complete sentence. Change capital letters and punctuation where necessary.

1. Jim, who is the best player on the team.

_____

2. Opened the package and put it carefully on the table.

_____

3. Jumped straight up and scored the basket.

_____

4. Changing the way we do things.

_____

5. Promised me I could have it for a week.

_____

• Correct each of the fragments below by connecting it to the accompanying sentence. Change capital letters and punctuation where necessary.

1. Many people don't like abstract art. Because they don't understand it.

_____

2. The abstract movement was started by a number of gifted artists. Like Miró and Kandinsky.

_____

3. They thought art was becoming too realistic. Looking just like photography.

_____

4. Some photographers also joined. Looking for new ways to see the world.

_____

Run-ons

> **A run-on is two or more complete sentences written without proper punctuation between them.**
>
> Run-ons: Ballet is exhausting work, you have to be in great shape to be a dancer.
>
>   It looks easy it's really hard.
>
>   It's beautiful, though, ballet is my favorite activity.
>
> **Run-ons can be corrected in three ways.**
>
> **1. If the two sentences are closely related, they can be separated by a semi-colon.**
>
> Correct: Ballet is exhausting work; you have to be in great shape to be a dancer.
>
> **2. Closely related sentences can also be separated with a comma and a conjunction.**
>
> Correct: It looks easy, but it's really hard.
>
> **3. Sentences that are not as closely related can be separated with a period.**
>
>   It's beautiful, though. Ballet is my favorite activity.

• Correct the run-ons below by rewriting the sentences correctly. If a sentence is not a run-on, write **OK** next to it.

_____ 1. Studying leaves is fascinating there are so many different kinds.

_____

_____ 2. Leaves come in different shades of green no two kinds seem to be the same.

_____

_____ 3. Leaves that grow in low light are usually dark green leaves that grow in bright light are lighter green.

_____

_____ 4. A leaf's shape is important experts can tell a lot about a tree from the shape of its leaves.

_____

_____ 5. Leaves from rain forest plants often have drip tips these are pointed tips that help water run off the leaf.

_____

_____ 6. Some leaves have complicated shapes these shapes allow the wind to blow the leaf without tearing it.

_____

_____ 7. Desert plants' leaves often have a waxy coating this helps them to conserve water.

_____

_____ 8. Hormones and the amount of daylight a plant receives can affect plant growth.

_____

Inverted Sentence Order

> **Sometimes part or all of the verb comes before the subject in a sentence. Sentences in which this happens are called inverted sentences. Inverted means that the order is reversed.**
>
> <u>Is</u> Bill <u>finished</u> with the dictionary?
>
> On the corner <u>is</u> the best ice-cream store in town.
>
> <u>Have</u> you <u>heard</u> the new CD yet?
>
> If you had trouble finding the subject and predicate in any of those sentences, try rearranging the subject and predicate.
>
> Bill <u>is finished</u> with the dictionary.
>
> The best ice-cream store in town <u>is</u> on the corner.
>
> You <u>have heard</u> the new CD yet.

• In each of the following sentences, draw one line under the simple subject and two lines under the verb.

1. What is the capital of Australia?

2. Isn't it Canberra?

3. In the hills near Canberra is the prettiest scenery in Australia.

4. Nearby are the homes of koalas and wombats.

5. There is the home of the kookaburra, also.

6. Here is a map of Australia.

7. Will you ever go to Australia?

8. Have you been there?

9. Aren't there rain forests on the Queensland coast?

10. Off the Queensland coast is the Great Barrier Reef.

11. Is Australia a country as well as a continent?

12. With whom does Australia trade?

Recognizing Nouns

> **Nouns are words that name people, places, things, or ideas. Nouns are words that identify—that person is *John*, that place is *home*, that thing is a *ball*, or that idea is *responsibility*.**
>
> kite, president, bell, book, candle, freedom, ships, shoes, democracy, Crazy Horse, doctor, house, park

• Below each of the nouns, write whether the noun names a person, place, thing, or idea.

1. rock

2. firefighter

3. China

4. book

5. Lucy Van Pelt

6. jet

7. Michigan

8. pen

9. tree

10. rage

11. Rachel Carson

12. boat

13. happiness

14. Tennessee

15. joy

16. emotion

> **The words *a*, *an*, and *the* are often used before nouns. These words are known as articles.**

• Write the correct article (**a** or **an**) to go with each of the nouns below. If the noun begins with a consonant sound, use the article **a**. If the noun begins with a vowel sound, use the article **an**. Remember, it is the sound not the spelling which helps you make this determination.

_____ book   _____ eagle   _____ sea   _____ President

_____ hour   _____ tiger   _____ keyboard   _____ idea

_____ classroom   _____ penguin   _____ exclamation   _____ opera

• Write a short paragraph about an issue that is in the news. Underline each noun that you use.

_____

_____

_____

_____

_____

Recognizing Nouns: Suffixes

> **A word ending is called a suffix. The following suffixes are sometimes used to end nouns: *-hood, -dom, -ment, -ance, -ness, -er, -or*.**
>
> childhood, earldom, excitement, appearance, illness, teacher, animator

• Use a suffix to create a noun from each of the words below.

1. drive	5. still	9. king	13. amuse
2. adult	6. sick	10. parent	14. bore
3. neighbor	7. govern	11. firm	15. sing
4. free	8. attend	12. happy	16. encourage

• Circle the suffix in each of the nouns below. Write a sentence for each of the nouns.

1. statehood

_____

2. insurance

_____

3. player

_____

4. operator

_____

5. establishment

_____

6. brightness

_____

7. performance

_____

8. avoidance

_____

9. happiness

_____

  IF8732 Grammar 7–8

Common and Proper Nouns

Proper nouns are the names of particular persons, places, or things. They are spelled with capital letters. Your name is a proper noun.

New York City, Babe Ruth, Clara Barton,
Empire State Building

All other nouns are called common nouns. Common nouns do not name particular persons, places, or things.

city, athlete, nurse, building

• If the word listed below is a proper noun, write the common noun that describes it. If it is a common noun, give an example of a proper noun that matches the word. Underline the proper noun in each pair of words.

Examples: <u>Babe Ruth</u>: athlete
city: <u>Los Angeles</u>

1. car: _____

2. teacher: _____

3. Abraham Lincoln: _____

4. Mayflower: _____

5. country: _____

6. Michael: _____

7. girl: _____

8. Big Mac: _____

9. Dan Rather: _____

10. actress: _____

11. Mark Twain: _____

12. constellation: _____

13. Buddhism: _____

14. Mt. Everest: _____

15. St. Louis: _____

16. *New York Times*: _____

• Choose five sets of nouns above. For each pair of words, write one sentence that uses both the proper and the common noun correctly.

1. _____

2. _____

3. _____

4. _____

5. _____

Abstract and Concrete Nouns

> **A concrete noun names something that can be seen or touched.**
> bridge, shell, car
> **An abstract noun names an idea, quality, or state of mind.**
> liberty, intelligence, happiness

- Label the following words as concrete (**C**) or abstract (**A**).

  _____ 1. fence

  _____ 2. success

  _____ 3. Dr. Smith

  _____ 4. sadness

  _____ 5. research

  _____ 6. desk

  _____ 7. Columbia River

  _____ 8. hat

  _____ 9. walnuts

  _____ 10. imagination

  _____ 11. forgetfulness

  _____ 12. telephone

- In the following sentences circle the concrete nouns and underline the abstract nouns.

  1. Mount Everest, located in Tibet, is the highest mountain on earth.

  2. Tibetan nomads must exert a lot of energy in their daily struggle to live.

  3. One skill they possess is horsemanship.

  4. Becoming a Buddhist monk is considered a high honor among the Tibetan people.

  5. The Dalai Lama, Tibet's leader, is considered an inspiration to his people.

  6. Tibet has far fewer monasteries today than it did in the past.

  7. The monks in the monasteries encourage education, art, and worship.

- List three abstract nouns and three concrete nouns.

  1. (abstract) _____

  2. (abstract) _____

  3. (abstract) _____

  1. (concrete) _____

  2. (concrete) _____

  3. (concrete) _____

Plural Nouns

> **Plural means more than one. To form the plural of most nouns, just add -s.**
>
> book, books; time, times; house, houses; lesson, lessons
>
> **If a noun ends in *s, x, ch, z, sh,* or *ss,* add -es.**
>
> bus, buses; fox, foxes; lunch, lunches; waltz, waltzes; dish, dishes; boss, bosses

- Write sentences using the plural forms of the nouns listed.

1. pilot, airplane

   _____

2. box, square

   _____

3. team, bus

   _____

4. boss, job

   _____

5. window, tree

   _____

6. book, class

   _____

7. batter, hit

   _____

8. cloud, wish

   _____

9. lesson, suffix

   _____

10. branch, root

    _____

- Write three sentences, each of which includes at least one singular noun and one plural noun. Underline the singular nouns and circle the plural nouns.

   1. _____

   2. _____

   3. _____

More Plural Nouns

To form the plural of nouns that end in a _y_ preceded by a consonant, change the _y_ to _i_ and add -_es_.
   baby, babies

For nouns that end in a _y_ preceded by a vowel, just add -_s_.
   key, keys

To form the plural of a word that ends in an _o_ preceded by a vowel, add -_s_. For words that end in an _o_ preceded by a consonant, usually add -_es_. (Check a dictionary if you're unsure.)
   folio, folios; tomato, tomatoes

For words that end in _f_ or _fe_, sometimes change the _f_ to _v_ and add -_es_; other times just add -_s_ (Consult a dictionary if you're unsure.)
   knife, knives; safe, safes; chief, chiefs

• Write the plural form next to each singular noun in the list below.

1. monkey _____
2. class _____
3. tax _____
4. berry _____
5. loaf _____
6. latch _____
7. fez _____
8. wish _____
9. hoof _____
10. galley _____
11. shoe _____
12. wax _____

13. horse _____
14. roof _____
15. puff _____
16. honey _____
17. color _____
18. waltz _____
19. wife _____
20. victory _____
21. potato _____
22. tress _____
23. story _____
24. avocado _____

Note: There are some words that don't follow any rules—their plurals just have to be learned. For instance, _deer_ and _species_ are spelled the same whether singular or plural. Feeling confused? When in doubt, always check your dictionary.

Check your dictionary and write the plural form for each of these nouns.

1. crisis _____
2. brother-in-law _____
3. man _____

4. ox _____
5. spoonful _____
6. datum _____

Gender of Nouns

Gender refers to the sex indicated by the noun. The four genders are masculine, which indicates the male sex; feminine, which indicates the female sex; neuter, which indicates no sex; and indefinite, which means the gender could be either male or female.

  masculine—actor, king,
  feminine—actress, queen
  neuter—car, boat
  indefinite—assistant, teacher

- Label each noun below according to the correct gender. Write **M** for masculine, **F** for feminine, **N** for neuter, and **I** for indefinite.

_____ 1. carpet

_____ 2. knight

_____ 3. niece

_____ 4. filly

_____ 5. lamb

_____ 6. doorknob

_____ 7. waitress

_____ 8. grandmother

_____ 9. President

_____ 10. automobile

_____ 11. uncle

_____ 12. brother

_____ 13. dam

_____ 14. doctor

_____ 15. empress

_____ 16. giraffe

_____ 17. princess

_____ 18. goddess

_____ 19. gopher

_____ 20. jellyfish

_____ 21. heiress

_____ 22. gourmet

_____ 23. emperor

_____ 24. grandson

_____ 25. river

_____ 26. pitcher

_____ 27. goat

- Write a short paragraph explaining how a woman's position in society has changed in recent years. In your paragraph, place an **M** above the nouns that are masculine, an **F** above those that are feminine, an **N** above those that are neuter, and an **I** above those that are indefinite.

_____

_____

_____

_____

_____

Possessive Nouns

> **Nouns that show ownership are called possessive nouns.**
> **To form the possessive of a singular noun, add an apostrophe and an s (-'s).**
>   <u>Tom**'s**</u> bell, the <u>author**'s**</u> book, <u>society**'s**</u> values
>
> **To form the possessive of a plural noun, add only an apostrophe if the word ends in _s_.**
>   the <u>author**s'**</u> books, the <u>Norton**s'**</u> home
>
> **If the plural of the noun does not end in _s_, add an apostrophe and an s ('s).**
>   <u>men**'s**</u> race, <u>children**'s**</u> hour

• Write the possessive of the following nouns.

1. woman _____
2. mice _____
3. horses _____
4. girls _____
5. teacher _____
6. umbrella _____
7. princess _____
8. home _____
9. players _____
10. students _____
11. host _____
12. country _____

13. presidents _____
14. scissors _____
15. Schindler _____
16. leaves _____
17. witnesses _____
18. actress _____
19. statue _____
20. pants _____
21. river _____
22. company _____
23. nurse _____
24. states _____

• Write a short paragraph describing some of your and your family's favorite possessions. Underline the possessive nouns.

_____

_____

_____

_____

_____

Collective Nouns

A collective noun names a group of persons, places, or things.
   band, team, audience, United States
When a collective noun refers to the group as a unit, the noun is considered singular.
   The <u>family</u> went on vacation.
   The <u>flock</u> headed on its northern course.
When a collective noun refers to the individual members of the group who are acting separately, the noun is considered plural.
   The <u>class</u> brought their pets to show and tell.
   The <u>family</u> are all going their separate ways.

• Indicate whether the collective nouns in the following sentences are singular **(S)** or plural **(P)**. Circle the correct word if there is a choice to be made.

_____ 1. The jury filed out of the courtroom.

_____ 2. The family (is, are) going on vacation to Georgia.

_____ 3. All during the game the crowd (was, were) very enthusiastic.

_____ 4. The team (is, are) getting on the bus after (its, their) heartbreaking loss.

_____ 5. The school staff worked throughout the summer on (its, their) lesson plans.

_____ 6. That group of spectators (is, are) getting awfully rowdy.

_____ 7. The symphony (is, are) playing some of the old favorites.

_____ 8. The set of books fell from the shelf.

_____ 9. The audience (is, are) returning to (its, their) cars.

_____ 10. The staff (was, were) happy about (its, their) bonuses.

• Write a short paragraph using at least three collective nouns. Write **P** or **S** above each collective noun to show if it is singular or plural.

_____

_____

_____

_____

_____

Predicate Nouns

A predicate noun is a noun used as a subject complement. Predicate nouns follow linking verbs.

Theodore Roosevelt was the <u>President</u> back then.

• In each of the following sentences, circle the linking verb and underline the predicate noun.

1. After his retirement, Mark became a consultant.

2. Uncle Earl was the best storyteller in the family.

3. Ben is a talented student.

4. Rick was president of the club last year.

5. St. Paul is the capital of Minnesota.

6. "The Raven" is the most popular poem in the anthology.

7. Mildred became an authority on fungi.

8. The President is the commander in chief.

9. Alaska became part of the United States in this century.

10. Melissa was a talented sculptor.

11. Grandfather became a carpenter.

12. The principal is chairperson of the committee.

13. The general was the leader of the army.

14. The boy was a soldier in the Civil War.

• Write four sentences using predicate nouns. Underline the predicate nouns.

1. _____

2. _____

3. _____

4. _____

Direct Objects

> **A direct object is a noun or pronoun that follows an action verb. It tells what or who receives the action of the verb.**
>
> The flood washed out the <u>road</u>.
>
> **To find the direct object, ask *who* or *what* after the action verb.**
>
> Question: The flood washed out *what*?
>
> Answer: the *road* (direct object)

- In each of the following sentences, circle the action verb and underline the direct object.

1. The Polar Bears won the championship.

2. Darcy answered the question.

3. Without delay Jasper boarded the train.

4. The salesclerk in the department store sold every pink shirt in stock.

5. President Lincoln sent General Grant into the battle.

6. The student read the newspaper every day.

7. The three networks immediately sent reporters to the crime scene.

8. Marcel gave a check to the charitable organization.

9. The principal grabbed the basketball.

10. Father wants us to return the car as soon as possible.

11. The French teacher sponsors the Honor Society.

12. The enthusiastic boy joined the team.

13. Julie won the prize at the fair last summer.

14. The clown wearing the polka-dotted hat threw the balloon.

15. He chose us to go on the trip with Harry.

- Write three sentences, including a noun used as a direct object in each. Underline the direct object and circle the action verb.

_____

_____

_____

Indirect Objects

> An indirect object is a noun or pronoun that names the person *to whom* or *for whom* something is done.
>
> Martina served the <u>guests</u> raw fish.
>
> **To find the indirect object, ask *to whom* or *for whom* after the action verb.**
>
> Question: Martina served raw fish *to whom*?
> Answer: the *guests* (indirect object)

• In each of the following sentences, underline the indirect object and circle the action verb.

1. Paul told him the bad news.

2. The director taught the choir a new song.

3. Gerald gave Sharon a symbol of his love.

4. I sent Barbara a postcard from France.

5. The farmer fed the geese the corn.

6. The star goalie left her two tickets at the gate.

7. The boss handed his employee the broom.

8. The book won her instant fame.

9. The window in the office offered the clients a good view.

10. Mary offered the secretary a piece of cake.

11. Shelly gave them her trophy to put in the display case.

• Write three sentences, including an indirect object in each. Underline the indirect objects once, the direct objects twice, and circle the action verbs.

1. _____

2. _____

3. _____

Objects of Prepositions

> **A noun or pronoun used as the object of a preposition follows the preposition, though there may be modifiers of the noun coming between it and the preposition.**
>   She waited <u>in the *building*</u>.
>   Marie gave the book <u>to *him.*</u>
> **To find the object, ask *whom* or *what* after the preposition.**
>   She waited in *what*? the *building*
>   Marie gave the book to *whom*? to *him*

• In each sentence, underline the entire prepositional phrase and circle the object of the preposition.

1. We all hoped for something exciting under the Christmas tree.

2. Santa's sleigh flew over the house.

3. Sara scurried into a hiding place she always reserved for herself.

4. I told her it was just St. Nick on the roof.

5. Her response was to crawl farther under her bed.

6. Now we could hear him in the kitchen.

7. Then I wondered why he was in that part of the house.

8. Just to be safe, I looked in the phone book and dialed the police.

9. Santa found a turkey sandwich in the refrigerator.

10. We had forgotten to put out cookies for him.

11. He was gone when the police pulled onto the driveway.

• Write three sentences about a holiday. Each sentence should include a prepositional phrase. Underline the entire prepositional phrase and circle the object of the preposition.

1. _____

2. _____

3. _____

Appositives

An appositive is a noun or noun phrase placed next to or very near another noun or noun phrase to identify, explain, or supplement its meaning.

Mr. Lange, <u>our English teacher</u>, is very intelligent.

• In each of the following sentences, underline the appositive and circle the noun it explains.

1. Kerri, my older sister, left immediately.

2. His car, a vintage roadster, crashed.

3. That man, the village chief, will command.

4. Baseball, my favorite sport, ended yesterday.

5. The senator, a Democrat, voted today.

6. Mr. Tobias, our Latin teacher, was nominated and defeated.

7. His house, a rambling shack, burned down.

8. The dog, a huge German shepherd, jumped up.

9. The boat, a sleek cruiser, slid past.

10. My cat, a grey manx, stretched and yawned.

11. Did you see the film at Studio 28, the movie theater?

12. My favorite ice cream, butter pecan, was on sale.

• Write three sentences which include appositives about three famous people currently in the news.

1. _____

2. _____

3. _____

Recognition of Verbs

A verb is a word that expresses action or a state of being.
  action—run, fish, swim, travel, stumble
  state of being—looks, is, were, seems

• In each of the following sentences, circle the verb and indicate if it is an action verb **(A)** or a state of being verb **(B)**.

_____ 1. Powerful telescopes probe the remote reaches of the universe.

_____ 2. New technology strips away old limitations.

_____ 3. Computers adjust the optics.

_____ 4. Hawaii's Keck Telescope is amazing.

_____ 5. The Milky Way is an example of a spiral galaxy.

_____ 6. The Milky Way contains hundreds of billions of stars.

_____ 7. A supernova is an exploding star.

_____ 8. A lot of knowledge about the galaxy is pure conjecture.

• Identify these verbs as action verbs **(A)** or state of being verbs **(B)**.

_____ 1. <u>hugs</u> the child   _____ 5. <u>am</u> sorry   _____ 9. <u>read</u> a book

_____ 2. <u>was</u> a pilot   _____ 6. <u>lifted</u> the bar   _____ 10. <u>sings</u> the song

_____ 3. <u>threw</u> the ball   _____ 7. <u>seems</u> cold   _____ 11. <u>looks</u> pretty

_____ 4. <u>baked</u> a cake   _____ 8. <u>mail</u> the letter   _____ 12. <u>is</u> happy

• Write three sentences that contain action verbs and three that contain state of being verbs. Underline the action verbs once and the state of being verbs twice.

1. (action) _____

2. (action) _____

3. (action) _____

4. (being) _____

5. (being) _____

6. (being) _____

More Verbs

> **A verb is a word that expresses action or a state of being.**

- In each of the following sentences, circle the verb and tell if it is an action verb (**A**) or a state of being verb (**B**).

_____ 1. Macaws are the largest of all parrots.

_____ 2. Their very long tails are unique in the parrot family.

_____ 3. Their wings are long and pointed.

_____ 4. Macaws eat fruit, nuts, and seeds.

_____ 5. The macaw screams loudly.

_____ 6. The macaw's coloring is spectacular.

_____ 7. The Scarlet macaw is the best known species.

_____ 8. Eighteen species of these parrots live in South America.

_____ 9. These birds are often poached.

_____ 10. People easily tame macaws.

_____ 11. Macaws' big beaks are extremely powerful.

_____ 12. These birds fly swiftly over the rain forest.

_____ 13. These large parrots nest in the holes of trees.

_____ 14. They are not common household pets.

_____ 15. Macaws live in forested areas.

- Write a short paragraph about a pet you would like to have. Include action and state of being verbs and circle them.

_____

_____

_____

_____

Active Voice Verbs

> **A verb is in the active voice when the subject is performing the action. (The subject is underlined once; the verb, twice.)**
>
> <u>Ron</u> <u><u>changed</u></u> his clothes.
> The <u>elephant</u> <u><u>fell</u></u> from the stand.
> The <u>stone</u> <u><u>shattered</u></u> his glasses.

• Each of these sentences contains an active verb. Underline the simple subject once and the verb twice.

1. Amelia Earhart flew alone over the Atlantic Ocean.

2. She made her crossing in 1932.

3. Amelia opened the field of aviation for many other women.

4. Ms. Earhart worked as a nurse's aide during World War I.

5. She earned a pilot's license by 1922.

6. She married George Putnam, a publisher.

7. This brave pilot tried to fly around the world in 1937.

8. Her plane disappeared during a flight over the Pacific Ocean.

9. Her mysterious disappearance fueled much speculation over the years.

10. Some people believe she drowned.

11. Her navigator also vanished.

• Write five sentences using active verbs about a trip you have taken. Underline the simple subjects once and the verbs twice.

1. _____

2. _____

3. _____

4. _____

5. _____

Passive Voice Verbs

> **A verb is in the passive voice when the subject is receiving the action. (The subject is underlined once; the verb, twice.)**
>
> The <u>windows</u> <u>were cleaned</u> by Roger.
> The <u>house</u> <u>was painted</u> by professionals.
> A lot of <u>homework</u> <u>was given</u> by the teacher.

• Change the following sentences using active verbs instead of passive verbs.

1. The people of France had been ruled by the aristocracy for centuries.

   _____

2. Louis XVI was blamed by the common people for new, burdensome taxes.

   _____

3. In 1789 a royal fortress called the Bastille was stormed by a mob of angry Parisians.

   _____

4. Royal troops were forced by the mob to withdraw from Paris.

   _____

5. Later, the revolutionary French government was overthrown by Napoleon Bonaparte.

   _____

6. The central government was made strong through Napoleon's efficient administration.

   _____

7. Europe was nearly destroyed by Napoleon's ambition.

   _____

8. Napoleon was finally defeated by his enemies at the Battle of Waterloo.

   _____

9. The rest of Europe also was influenced by the French Revolution.

   _____

• Write three sentences using passive verbs about an event in history.

1. _____

2. _____

3. _____

Using Active and Passive Voice Verbs

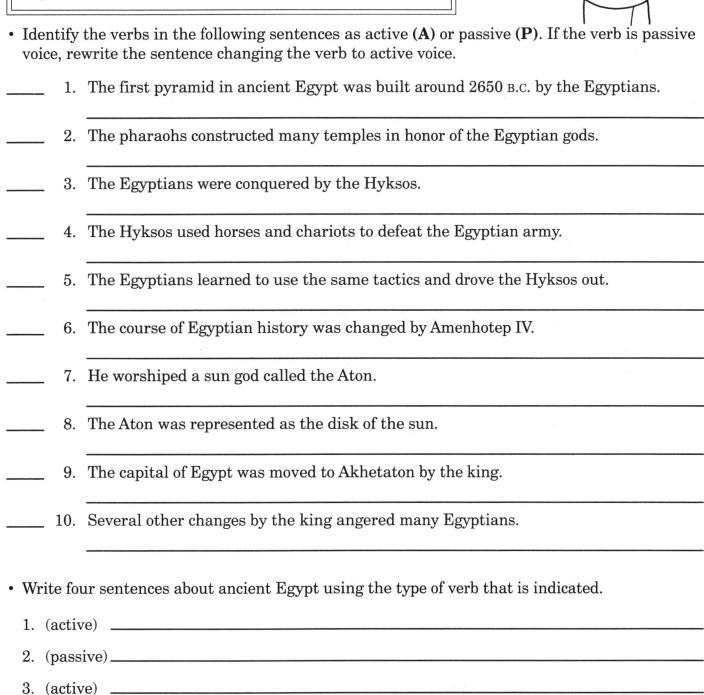

A verb is in the active voice when the subject performs the action. A verb is in the passive voice when the subject receives the action.

Passive voice should be used sparingly. Active voice expresses action in a natural, more direct way.

- Identify the verbs in the following sentences as active **(A)** or passive **(P)**. If the verb is passive voice, rewrite the sentence changing the verb to active voice.

_____ 1. The first pyramid in ancient Egypt was built around 2650 B.C. by the Egyptians.

_____

_____ 2. The pharaohs constructed many temples in honor of the Egyptian gods.

_____

_____ 3. The Egyptians were conquered by the Hyksos.

_____

_____ 4. The Hyksos used horses and chariots to defeat the Egyptian army.

_____

_____ 5. The Egyptians learned to use the same tactics and drove the Hyksos out.

_____

_____ 6. The course of Egyptian history was changed by Amenhotep IV.

_____

_____ 7. He worshiped a sun god called the Aton.

_____

_____ 8. The Aton was represented as the disk of the sun.

_____

_____ 9. The capital of Egypt was moved to Akhetaton by the king.

_____

_____ 10. Several other changes by the king angered many Egyptians.

_____

- Write four sentences about ancient Egypt using the type of verb that is indicated.

1. (active) _____

2. (passive) _____

3. (active) _____

4. (passive) _____

Verb Phrases

> **A verb phrase is a group of words that does the work of a single verb. The phrase includes one principal verb and one or more helping verbs.**
> The teacher <u>was trying</u> to control the class.

• In each of the following sentences, underline the verb phrase and circle the helping verbs.

1. Charles Darwin was born in 1809.

2. He was raised in Shrewsbury, England.

3. The theory of evolution was introduced by Charles Darwin in the 1850s.

4. Many people are attracted by the logic of the theory.

5. The theory has been refined over the years.

6. Darwin was exploring on the H.M.S. *Beagle* in 1831.

7. He had studied plant and animal life on his travels.

8. He was forming an explanation for the phenomena he observed.

9. His theory was supported by Alfred Russell Wallace, a noted British scientist.

10. Darwin was convinced that modern species evolved from earlier ones.

11. He was fascinated by the process of natural selection.

12. His place in history was strengthened by his book *The Origin of Species*.

13. Darwin's work has had influence on religious thought.

14. Many people have opposed his theories.

15. Other writers and scientists have referred to Darwin's ideas in their own work.

• Write four sentences about geography which contain verb phrases. Underline the verb phrases and circle the helping verbs.

1. _____

2. _____

3. _____

4. _____

Regular Verbs

> **A regular verb is one which forms its past tense and past participle by adding *-d* or *-ed* to the present tense form.**
>   walk, walked, (have/has/had) walked
>   try, tried, (have/has/had) tried
>   call, called, (have/has/had) called

• Write the past and the past participle forms of the following verbs.

Present	Past	Past Participle
1. crawl	_____	(have, has, had) _____
2. skate	_____	(have, has, had) _____
3. fish	_____	(have, has, had) _____
4. climb	_____	(have, has, had) _____
5. love	_____	(have, has, had) _____
6. answer	_____	(have, has, had) _____
7. travel	_____	(have, has, had) _____
8. contend	_____	(have, has, had) _____
9. pretend	_____	(have, has, had) _____
10. develop	_____	(have, has, had) _____

• Use each of the following verbs in a sentence of your own.

1. derive _____

2. has commanded _____

3. have served _____

4. open _____

5. has watched _____

6. rule _____

7. have crashed _____

8. jump _____

9. has realized _____

Irregular Verbs

An irregular verb is any verb which does not form
its past and past participle by adding *-d* or *-ed* to its
present tense.

> begin, began, (has, have, had) begun
> lead, led, (has, have, had) led
> grow, grew, (has, have, had) grown

• Write the past and past participle forms of the following verbs.

Present	Past		Past Participle
1. freeze	_____	(have, has, had)	_____
2. break	_____	(have, has, had)	_____
3. fight	_____	(have, has, had)	_____
4. become	_____	(have, has, had)	_____
5. see	_____	(have, has, had)	_____
6. shake	_____	(have, has, had)	_____
7. give	_____	(have, has, had)	_____
8. eat	_____	(have, has, had)	_____
9. take	_____	(have, has, had)	_____
10. wear	_____	(have, has, had)	_____

• Use each of the following verbs to write a sentence of your own. Underline the present tense
verbs once, the past tense verbs twice, and the past participle tense verbs three times.

1. drew _____

2. have gone _____

3. has frozen _____

4. creep _____

5. fell _____

6. has bitten _____

Linking Verbs

A linking verb does not show action. It connects a word or words in the predicate to the subject in the sentence. Some very common linking verbs are forms of *be*: am, are, is, was, were.

Father <u>is</u> a banker.
I <u>am</u> a student.

- In each of the following sentences, underline the linking verb and circle the two words that are joined by it.

  1. Water is part of all living things.

  2. Water molecules are simple in structure.

  3. Water management is a complex problem.

  4. A desert is a hot, barren region.

  5. Desert living is common.

  6. Farming is restricted.

  7. Rainfall is scarce.

  8. Water for cities is sometimes difficult to find.

  9. States which lack water supplies are often desperate for help.

  10. Nearby rivers are sources of water.

  11. It is important to consider the ecological effects of any diversion of water.

  12. Some desert areas are cold.

  13. Most deserts are very hot.

  14. The largest desert is the Sahara.

- Write four sentences about the geography of your state using a linking verb in each.

  1. _____

  2. _____

  3. _____

  4. _____

More Linking Verbs

> A linking verb does not show action. It connects a word or words in the predicate to the subject in the sentence. Forms of *be* are common linking verbs. Other linking verbs include *grow, look, became, appear, look, taste,* and *remain*.
>
> **Note: A verb is a linking verb if you can substitute the verb "is" or "was" for it.**
> "The food <u>tasted</u> spicy."   "The food <u>was</u> spicy."

- In each of the following sentences, underline the linking verb and circle the two words that are joined by it.

    1. A mountain lion remains a common sight in western parts of the United States.

    2. The puma is a mountain lion.

    3. The lioness walking through the grass looked powerful.

    4. When people approach, the puma becomes secretive.

    5. To some ranchers the panther became a nuisance.

    6. Their extinction seemed possible.

    7. Environmentalists became interested in their plight.

    8. The puma is a territorial animal.

    9. This information became crucial to help save the animal.

   10. Today the puma is plentiful again.

- Write sentences of your own using the linking verbs listed below. Remember to test your verb choice by seeing if you can substitute "is" or "was" for the linking verb.

    1. grow _____

    2. has felt _____

    3. seems _____

    4. tasted _____

    5. has remained _____

    6. was _____

Transitive Verbs

> A transitive verb is an action verb that is followed by a direct object. The verb "transmits" the action from the subject to the object.
> The (teacher) <u>graded</u> three (papers).

- In each of the following sentences underline the transitive verb and circle the subject and direct object.

1. The fire cast dancing shadows across the room.

2. The choir bought new outfits for the concert.

3. The sleigh rails hit the roof with a loud bang.

4. Rodney handled the flaming torch with ease.

5. The disc jockey picked a song from the list.

6. The outfielder hit the wall with a thud.

7. The goalie stopped the ball.

8. The horse jumped the obstacle with ease.

9. Kenny slugged the baseball into the outfield.

10. He served the tennis ball over the net.

11. The woman painted the room.

12. Charlie washed the windows.

13. My friend types 80 words per minute.

14. The toddler slammed the cupboard drawer on his fingers.

- Write four sentences about a party. Be sure to use transitive verbs. Underline the transitive verbs and circle the direct objects.

1. _____

2. _____

3. _____

4. _____

Intransitive Verbs

An intransitive verb does not need an object to complete its meaning. It is frequently followed by a prepositional phrase.

The tower <u>collapsed</u> to the ground.

• In each of the following sentences, underline the intransitive verb and circle the subject.

1. The city of Jerusalem is located near the center of Israel.

2. The control of the city of Jerusalem has changed often over the centuries.

3. The city was captured by King David.

4. Under his rule the city flourished.

5. However, it was sacked by the Babylonians in 587 or 586 B.C.

6. The great Temple of Jerusalem was built by King Solomon.

7. The Temple was destroyed.

8. Jewish people gather every day at the Wailing Wall.

9. A mosque, the Dome of the Rock, was built on the same site.

10. On a nearby site a Christian holy place, the Church of the Holy Sepulcher, stands.

11. Jerusalem is revered by Jews, Christians, and Muslims.

12. Throughout history tensions have arisen between the groups.

13. Many plans for resolving the disputes have failed.

14. All signs in the city are printed in three languages—Hebrew, Arabic, and English.

15. Pilgrims come from all over the world to Jerusalem.

• Write five sentences about your city or one that you have visited. Include an intransitive verb in each sentence. Underline the intransitive verbs and circle the subjects.

1. _____

2. _____

3. _____

4. _____

5. _____

Simple Tenses

The tense of a verb indicates the time an action takes place.
  Present tense indicates action or being that is happening now.
    Susan <u>loves</u> ice cream. She <u>is</u> here.
  Past tense indicates action or being that was completed in the past.
    Matthew <u>loved</u> the new movie. He <u>was</u> here.
  Future tense indicates action or being that will take place in the future. The auxiliary verbs *will* and *shall* are used with the principal verb to form the future tense.
    Ellen <u>will love</u> this house. She <u>will be</u> here tomorrow.

• Identify the tense of the verb in each sentence: present tense **(P)**, past tense **(PA)**, or future tense **(F)**. Then rewrite the sentence using another tense.

_____ 1. I will hike to the top of the mountain.

_____ 2. He fought against the onslaught of mosquitoes.

_____ 3. Daniel compared this trip to others.

_____ 4. They wear all the standard gear.

_____ 5. We shall elect a leader!

_____ 6. Naomi was an excellent survivalist.

_____ 7. She swept through the underbrush.

_____ 8. They will collect samples of leaves along the way.

_____ 9. The groups return to camp each evening.

• Write one sentence in each simple tense about a camping trip.

  1. (present) _____

  2. (past) _____

  3. (future) _____

Imperative Mood

The mood of the verb indicates the attitude or viewpoint behind the verb's expression. The imperative mood indicates a command or a request. The subject is always "you," though this is rarely expressed.

Please, close the door.

(Notice that "you" is understood to be the subject of this sentence.)

• Use the verbs below to write sentences of your own which are in the imperative mood.

1. check _____

2. return _____

3. wash _____

4. deliver _____

5. develop _____

6. count _____

7. drive _____

8. climb _____

9. send _____

10. take _____

11. stop _____

12. catch _____

• Write three sentences in the imperative mood that you might hear your principal or teacher say. Underline the verbs.

1. _____

2. _____

3. _____

• Put an **I** by the sentences written in the imperative mood.

_____ 1. The boy threw the baseball.

_____ 2. Sit here, please.

_____ 3. That movie was thoroughly enjoyable.

_____ 4. Step up here right now.

_____ 5. Pass the paper to me.

_____ 6. I love to paint with watercolors.

_____ 7. The windows need to be washed.

_____ 8. Park the car.

Agreement of Subject and Verb

> **A verb must agree with its subject in number. That is, a singular subject requires a singular verb, and a plural subject requires a plural verb.**
>
> Singular: The <u>tree</u> <u>sways</u> in the wind.
>
> Plural: The <u>trees</u> <u>sway</u> in the wind.
>
> **Note:** The number of the subject is not changed by a phrase or clause which might follow it.
>
> The <u>tree</u> with dozens of coconuts <u>sways</u> in the wind.
>
> The <u>trees</u> on this island <u>sway</u> in the wind.

• Circle the correct verb choice in each of the sentences below.

1. A single lightning bolt (is, are) capable of doing a great deal of damage.

2. The peak temperature of a bolt (heats, heat) the surrounding air to over 60,000°F.

3. The lightning stroke (create, creates) a jagged picture across the sky.

4. Commercial jets (is, are) seldom hit by lightning.

5. If struck, they (suffer, suffers) only slight damage.

6. Planes (has, have) special shielding to protect their electronic equipment.

7. Rocket launches (provide, provides) the best chance to study lightning.

8. Photography (is, are) another way to study lightning.

9. Scientists in many labs (think, thinks) that there is even lightning on Venus.

10. A bolt of lightning from the clouds (is, are) always an awesome sight.

• Write a short paragraph describing what it would be like to be caught out in a boat during a storm. Underline each verb and circle each subject.

_____

_____

_____

_____

_____

_____

Problem Verbs—Lie/Lay

Lie means to recline, to rest, or to remain in a reclining position. The principal parts of the verb *lie* are *lie, lay,* (*have, has, had*) *lain*. This verb never takes an object in any of its forms. There is no form of this verb ending in *d*. *Lie* is sometimes confused with the verb *lay,* which means to put something down or to place something somewhere. Its principal parts are *lay, laid,* (*have, has, had*) *laid*. This verb always takes an object.

Examples of sentences using *lie* :
John *lies* down for an hour every day. *present*
John *lay* on the deck in the sun. (not laid) *past*
John *has lain* on the deck often. (not has laid) *past participle*

Examples of sentences using *lay*:
Fred *lays* linoleum for a department store. *present*
Fred *laid* linoleum all day. *past*
Fred *has laid* linoleum since he left high school. *past participle*

• Circle the correct verb in each of the following sentences.

1. He (lay, laid) down to take a nap.

2. Lennie has (lain, laid) carpet for that store for years.

3. Our dog (laid, lay) in the mud.

4. My aunt (lays, lies) on the sofa every morning.

5. The hen (laid, lay) an egg yesterday morning.

6. The injured animal (lay, laid) motionless.

7. I think I will (lay, lie) down and take a nap.

8. (Lay, Lie) that book down.

9. He had (lain, laid) the scissors on the table.

• Use the following verbs in sentences of your own.

1. lies (rests) _____

2. laid (put down) _____

3. lay (reclined) _____

Problem Verbs—Sit/Set

The verb *sit* means to assume a sitting position or to occupy a seat. The principal parts of the verb *sit* are *sit, sat, (have, has, had) sat*. The verb *sit* never takes an object. This verb is sometimes confused with the verb *set*, which means to put something in position or to make something rigid. The principal parts of the verb *set* are *set, set, (have, has, had) set*. The verb *set* usually has an object.

Examples of sentences using *sit*:

I sit in the shade whenever I can.

Jack sat still, waiting for the fish to bite.

The governor has sat in that chair for many meetings.

Examples of sentences using *set*:

Tony set the silverware on the table.

Yesterday, Wally set the clock after the storm.

The realtor has set his commission too high.

• Circle the correct verb in each of the following sentences.

1. He (set, sat) still while his hair was being cut.

2. You should always (sit, set) in good light when you read.

3. Grandpa likes to (sit, set) in the rocking chair.

4. We (set, sat) the correct time on the computer after the storm ended.

5. The little boy (set, sat) there looking depressed.

6. You may (sit, set) the book on the table.

7. Please (sit, set) here and relax while I try to find your book.

8. Let's (set, sit) here and watch the rain.

9. The boys (sat, set) on the roof.

10. Paula likes to (sit, set) in the easy chair.

11. The doctor (sat, set) his leg skillfully.

12. The painter (sat, set) his ladders against the building before mixing his paints.

• Use the following verbs in sentences of your own.

1. has set _____

2. sit _____

Problem Verbs—Rise/Raise

The verb *rise* means to ascend, to swell up, and to rise in value or force. The principal parts of the verb *rise* are *rise, rose, (have, has, had) risen*. The verb rise does not take an object. This verb is sometimes confused with the verb *raise*, which means to lift up something, to cause it to go up, to increase the amount, to collect a number of objects, or to breed and grow. Its principal parts are *raise, raised, (have, has, had) raised*. The verb *raise* always takes an object.

Examples of sentences using *rise*:

The sun rises in the east.

The rocket rose steadily into the atmosphere.

The tide had risen by morning.

Examples of sentences using *raise*:

Many farmers raise soybeans as a cash crop.

Sheila raised the flag.

The charismatic politician had raised a huge sum of money.

• Circle the correct verb in each of the following sentences.

1. The hot air balloon (raises, rises) into the blue sky.

2. The stock market (rose, raised) 30 points yesterday because of the President's announcement.

3. The granite cliffs (raise, rise) high above the valley.

4. The guerilla leader (raised, rose) a great army of support.

5. The flood waters (raised, rose) rapidly.

6. The coffee dealers (rose, raised) the price of coffee beans.

7. The soldier (rose, raised) the flag.

8. The wedding guests had (raised, risen) their glasses to sip champagne for a toast.

• Use the verbs below to write sentences of your own.

1. raise _____

2. rises _____

3. rose _____

4. had raised _____

Troublesome Verbs

• Fill in the missing principal parts of the irregular verbs in the chart.

Present Tense	Past Tense	Past Participle
shake	shook	(have, has, had) shaken
lead		(have, has, had) led
freeze	froze	(have, has, had)
eat		(have, has, had) eaten
wear		(have, has, had) worn
know	knew	(have, has, had)
blow		(have, has, had) blown
drown	drowned	(have, has, had) drowned
catch	caught	(have, has, had)

• Circle the correct verb in each of the following sentences.

1. Kendra (blow, blew) out the candles on her birthday cake.

2. You have (ate, eaten) all of the treats put out for the party.

3. What will you (wear, have worn) to the party tomorrow?

4. John (shook, shaked) his head.

5. I (knew, knowed) it was his birthday.

6. He almost (drowned, drownded) trying to bob for apples.

7. I did not know to where the path (leaded, led).

8. The pond has been (froze, frozen) for several weeks now.

9. Terry (catched, caught) a cold the day before the party.

10. I have (weared, worn) this dress before.

11. After an hour outside, the water in the pail had (frozen, froze).

• Use the verbs below to write sentences of your own.

1. ate _____

2. lead _____

3. have shaken _____

More Troublesome Verbs

• Fill in the missing principal parts of the irregular verbs in the chart.

Present Tense	Past Tense	Past Participle
become	became	(have, has, had) become
choose	chose	(have, has, had)
drink		(have, has, had) drunk
throw	threw	(have, has, had)
write	wrote	(have, has, had)
flow		(have, has, had) flowed
see	saw	(have, has, had)
swear		(have, has, had) sworn
climb		(have, has, had) climbed

• Circle the correct verb choices in the following sentences.

1. Roger has (swore, sworn) to tell the truth.

2. The rising river (flowed, flew) under the bridge.

3. Ursula (wrote, written) many interesting letters.

4. Sam (become, became) angry yesterday.

5. Paul (has, have) climbed that tree in the backyard many times.

6. He (saw, seen) that movie three times already.

7. I have (choosed, chosen) Michael to be on our team.

8. I (drunk, drank) all my milk, Mom!

9. The boy had (threw, thrown) the ball into the woods.

10. The knight (sweared, swore) his loyalty to the king.

11. Sara has (became, become) a wonderful cook.

12. We found that the juice had (flew, flowed) from the hole in the cup.

• Use the verbs below to write sentences of your own.

1. has seen _____

2. have written _____

3. have thrown _____

And More Troublesome Verbs

- Fill in the missing principal parts of the irregular verbs in the chart.

Present Tense	Past Tense	Past Participle
cut	cut	(have, has, had) cut
drag		(have, has, had) dragged
wring	wrung	(have, has, had)
weave		(have, has, had) woven
lend	lent	(have, has, had)
say	said	(have, has, had)
take		(have, has, had) taken
let	let	(have, has, had)
go		(have, has, had) gone

- Circle the correct verb in each of the following sentences.

1. She has (wove, woven) a beautiful pattern into that garment.

2. Harris (lent, lended) Jake a lot of money.

3. Bob (say, said) that he is not going to the game.

4. This whole thing has (taken, took) far too long already.

5. Ellen (wrung, wringed) the water from the rag.

6. Grandpa (went, gone) to the store yesterday.

7. Sara had (cut, cutted) the cake and grabbed a piece before anyone noticed.

8. We have (went, gone) to that restaurant before.

9. The gardener (drug, dragged) the heavy shrub to the truck.

- Use the verbs below to write sentences of your own.

1. have gone _____

2. let _____

3. has lent _____

4. wrung _____

5. had said _____

Persons of Pronouns

The person of a pronoun tells whether the pronoun being used is the speaker, the one spoken to, or the one spoken about.
— The first person refers to the one speaking.   <u>I</u> am speaking. — The second person refers to the one spoken to.   <u>You</u> are the one. — The third person refers to the person or thing spoken about.   <u>She/It</u> is beautiful.

• In each of the following sentences, identify the person of each underlined pronoun by writing **1**, **2**, or **3** in the parentheses at the end of each sentence.

1. <u>He</u> was a soldier in the Civil War. (   )

2. I would like <u>you</u> to study the chapter on the causes of the war. (   )

3. <u>We</u> must understand the problems left behind at the end of the war. (   )

4. Abraham Lincoln guided <u>it</u> through a very difficult time. (   )

5. <u>I</u> admire Ulysses S. Grant. (   )

6. <u>He</u> was a talented general. (   )

7. The war created many problems, but <u>it</u> also solved a most serious one—slavery. (   )

8. Have <u>you</u> studied the Civil War before? (   )

9. My history teacher was correct when <u>she</u> said this material was important to learn. (   )

10. <u>We</u> will soon learn a poem written during this time. (   )

• Circle each first person pronoun, underline each second person pronoun, and draw a rectangle around each third person pronoun.

  I   he   she   you   we   it

• Write one sentence using first person, one sentence using second person, and one using third person. Circle the pronouns which indicate the person.

1. (first person) _____

2. (second person) _____

3. (third person) _____

Personal Pronouns

> **A pronoun is a word that takes the place of a noun. A *personal pronoun* indicates the speaker (first person), the one spoken to (second person), or the one spoken about (third person).**
> First person pronouns: I, my, mine, me, we, our, ours, us
> Second person pronouns: you, your, yours
> Third person pronouns: he, she, it, his, her, hers, its, him, her,
>   they, their, theirs, them

• Place a number **1** above first person pronouns, a **2** above second person pronouns, and a **3** above third person pronouns in the following sentences.

1. We are going to study the life of Joan of Arc.

2. What do you think we will learn from this study?

3. When Joan of Arc was thirteen years old, she realized her life was going to change.

4. She became convinced that Charles VII, the King of France, needed her help to drive out

   the English soldiers.

5. If you had been there, you might have doubted Joan's ability to help.

6. When she was seventeen she finally talked to the king.

7. Joan had talked to a commander first, and he laughed at her.

8. They did not think she would be of any help.

9. She led them in battle and was victorious at the Battle of Orléans.

10. Eventually she was captured and held prisoner by the English.

11. They thought she was a witch and burned her at the stake on May 30, 1431.

12. We will probably never know all of the details of her exciting life.

13. Do you admire her?

14. I do admire her bravery.

• Write three sentences about a daring adventure on which you would like to embark. Use at least one personal pronoun in each sentence. Underline the personal pronouns.

1. _____

2. _____

3. _____

Number and Gender of Pronouns

A pronoun must agree with its antecedent (the noun it refers to) in number and gender. If the noun is singular, the pronoun must be singular. If the noun is plural, the pronoun must be plural. If the noun is masculine, the pronoun must be masculine. If the noun is feminine, the pronoun must be feminine. If the noun is neuter (neither sex indicated), the pronoun must also be neuter.

• In the following sentences, place an **S** under the pronouns that are singular and a **P** under those that are plural. Then put an **F** above the pronouns that are female, an **M** above those that are male, and an **N** above those that are neuter.

1. Mary is the first person I would invite to the party. She is fun to talk to.

2. The car veered to the left of the line. It then stopped suddenly.

3. Can you go to the mall with Sara and me? We are leaving at 1:00 P.M.

4. We slid down the water slide. It was a very fast ride.

5. Tony's idea of a good time is to sit in front of the TV all night. He doesn't even like to play basketball.

6. We saw the plane heading toward the airport. Dad and I both checked the time to see if it was late.

7. The pilot let Billy sit in the cockpit. Boy was he thrilled!

8. Have you ever flown on a plane? Would you like to fly?

• Write a pronoun to take the place of the following nouns.

1. shelter _____   6. mountain _____

2. soccer _____   7. bull _____

3. relatives _____   8. daffodils _____

4. men _____   9. trains _____

5. dolphins _____   10. ewe _____

Indefinite Pronouns

> An indefinite pronoun is one which refers generally, not specifically, to persons, places, or things. Some indefinite pronouns are always singular, some are always plural, and some may be either singular or plural.
>
> **Singular indefinite pronouns:** anybody, anyone, another, each, either, everybody, everyone, nobody, no one, neither, one, other, someone, somebody, everything, anything, something
>
> **Plural indefinite pronouns:** many, both, few, several, others
>
> **Indefinite pronouns that may be either singular or plural:** all, any, most, some, none
>
> **Remember:** The number of the subject of the sentence is not affected by any phrases or clauses that come between it and the verb.

• In each of the following sentences, circle the verb or helping verb that agrees in number with the indefinite pronoun subject.

1. Every one of the students (like, likes) to be challenged.

2. Some of the material in this book (is, are) interesting.

3. Either of the two sisters (is, are) willing to pay for the gift.

4. Many of the people (was, were) disgusted with the media coverage.

5. Neither of the two teams (deserve, deserves) to play in the finals.

6. Anyone who thinks they know the answer (has, have) to raise his or her hand.

7. Each of the monkeys in the cage (play, plays) to the audience.

8. Most of the rocks in the bag (is, are) worthless.

9. All of the fish in the creek (was, were) killed by the insecticide.

10. Everyone who is interested (is, are) welcome to sign up.

11. Everybody in the band (is, are) very talented.

12. All of us (wish, wishes) the best for your future.

13. Several of the women on the job site (was, were) given a raise.

14. Few teachers (has, have) been as energetic as she has been.

15. One elephant (has, have) done a tremendous amount of damage to the village.

Name _____

Possessive and Interrogative Pronouns

| **A possessive pronoun is one which indicates ownership or possession.** |
Possessive pronouns: my, mine, your, yours, his, her, hers, its, our, ours, their, theirs

- Circle the possessive pronouns in the following sentences.
  1. Her vacation was planned a long time in advance.
  2. My travel agent helped put together her itinerary.
  3. His office telephoned many hotels and motels around the country.
  4. He was asking about their best rate.
  5. One hotel sent a brochure of its services.
  6. He drove their van to the airport.
  7. Our airport is open all night.
  8. Is that suitcase hers?
  9. Those boxes are theirs.
  10. Our flight is delayed.

An interrogative pronoun introduces a question.
Interrogative pronouns: who, whom, whose, what, which

- Circle the interrogative pronoun in each of the following sentences.
  1. Who will win this game tonight?
  2. Which is your house?
  3. What are we having for dinner?
  4. To whom will the people of this country turn?
  5. Whose child is this?

- Use the following interrogative pronouns to write sentences of your own.
  1. what _____
  2. which _____
  3. whose _____
  4. who _____
  5. whom _____

Reflexive and Relative Pronouns

> **Reflexive pronouns are formed by adding *-self* or *-selves* to certain forms of personal pronouns.**
>
> First person reflexive pronouns:
>   myself, ourselves
> Second person reflexive pronouns:
>   yourself, yourselves
> Third person reflexive pronouns:
>   himself, herself, itself, themselves

- Circle the reflexive pronoun in each of the following sentences.

1. I will use all of my efforts to develop myself to the best of my ability.

2. Have you done all of the problems by yourself?

3. John prepared the meat by himself.

4. We must defend ourselves because no one else will.

5. You might find yourselves needing help one day.

6. Rachael knew herself well enough to know when to ask for help.

7. She watched herself on TV and felt foolish.

> **Relative pronouns are used to introduce groups of words that act as adjectives.**
>
> Relative pronouns: who, whose, whom, which, that

- Circle the relative pronouns.

1. A breakfast that includes fruit is often recommended by nutritionists.

2. People who eat a good breakfast are full of energy in the late morning hours.

3. The dietician in whom I have put my trust is planning my meals.

4. She showed me a low-fat diet that I must follow.

5. She is a person who always eats healthy foods.

6. The diet, which I started last night, is easy to follow.

7. My sister, who is very slender, can eat whatever she wants.

8. She can't understand a person like me who has to watch everything I eat.

     IF8732 Grammar 7–8

Subject and Object Pronouns

When a pronoun is the subject of the sentence, it is called a subject pronoun.

He caught the ball. (subject)

When a pronoun is used as the direct object, indirect object, or object of a preposition, it is called an object pronoun.

Sally saw us. (direct object)
Matthew throws us the balls. (indirect object)
Todd threw the ball to us. (object of preposition)

• Circle the pronouns used as subjects, and underline the pronouns used as objects.

1. We will never allow it to happen in this school.

2. After thinking about it carefully, he decided to go anyway.

3. Even though the fruit was spoiled, the grocer sold it at the same price.

4. They told us that this was going to be a very exciting day.

5. I decided how the money should be spent.

6. I wanted her to help me make the decision.

7. She refused to do this.

8. Harry wanted to buy it at the fruit stand.

9. They did not stock apricot jam there.

10. He told them about a grocery store located several blocks away.

11. Mark told me about a movie.

12. We chatted about it while walking to the store.

• Write a short paragraph about a visit to another country using at least three subject pronouns and three object pronouns.

_____

_____

_____

_____

_____

_____

_____

Pronouns Who/Whom

The use of the pronouns *who* and *whom* is determined by the pronoun's function in the clause. Generally, *who* is used as a subject of a sentence or clause.

Who baked the cake?
The boy who baked it lives next door to me.

Whom is used as a direct object or an object of a preposition.

Whom did you visit last week?
With whom did you travel?

• Circle the correct pronoun in each of the following sentences.

1. Mr. Hands is the one (who, whom) handles disciplinary matters.

2. Do you think he is one in (who, whom) you can put your trust?

3. Matthew is well acquainted with people (who, whom) will tell the truth.

4. Kent is the person with (who, whom) you should speak.

5. (Who, Whom) is waiting for me?

6. For (who, whom) do you think we should vote?

7. To (who, whom) do you wish to speak?

8. The girl (who, whom) we met is very intelligent.

9. Phyllis, (who, whom) is my youngest sister, is going to become a doctor.

10. The person to (who, whom) you spoke is no longer here.

11. (Who, Whom) went to the play?

12. With (who, whom) did you see the movie?

13. My brother, (who, whom) lives in Georgia, likes to jog.

14. (Who, Whom) is coming to the party?

• Using the pronouns **who** and **whom**, write a short paragraph about something that you have studied in American history.

_____

_____

_____

_____

_____

_____

Sentences with Modifiers

> The complete subject or complete predicate of a sentence usually contains other words or phrases called modifiers that add to the meaning of the sentence.
>
> The <u>cold</u> water dripped <u>slowly over the jagged edge</u>.

• In the following sentences, underline the subject modifiers once and the predicate modifiers twice.

1. The small boy ran very fast.

2. The huge, gray dog ran eagerly.

3. The talented magician bowed gracefully.

4. The distraught mother silently watched.

5. The excited boy collided with the dog.

6. The long-stemmed roses landed in a tangled mess on the floor.

7. The frightened cat in the window jumped wildly.

• Add modifiers to the simple subjects and predicates below and create interesting sentences. Don't forget to capitalize the first word of the sentence.

1. player won game _____

2. car drove _____

3. children played _____

4. birds flew _____

5. Michelangelo painted murals _____

6. Miss Brown explained problem _____

7. sun shines _____

8. summer means _____

9. lakes freeze _____

10. trees grow _____

Identifying Adjectives

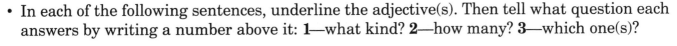

> An adjective modifies a noun or pronoun. It gives specific information by telling *what kind,* *how many,* or *which one.*
> green grass, two swimmers, this book

- In each of the following sentences, underline the adjective(s). Then tell what question each answers by writing a number above it: **1**—what kind? **2**—how many? **3**—which one(s)?

1. Ralph took his mangy, old dog for a long walk.

2. The dog, Joshua, reluctantly rose from the warm bricks in front of the blazing hearth.

3. He did not understand why anyone would want to venture out into the cold weather.

4. Ralph wore his bright red stocking cap pulled tightly over his big ears.

5. The cold air stung his red nose as he slogged through the blinding snow.

6. Those majestic pines were covered with a heavy layer of snow.

7. Joshua immediately had tiny icicles form in the fur of his four paws.

8. He stopped two times to try to remove the icy buildup.

9. When Ralph saw the pitiful look on Joshua's face, he knew he had made a mistake.

10. That dog endured the bitter wind.

11. He turned back to the warm house they had just left.

12. Joshua raced ahead to get back to the safe haven of his peaceful, toasty hearth.

13. Ralph peeled off the several layers of thick wool clothes and sat by the roaring fire.

14. He decided that the next time he took a long walk it would be a warm, spring day.

15. The faithful dog wagged his bushy tail.

- Write four sentences of your own using at least one adjective in each. Write about a summer day. Underline the adjectives.

1. _____

2. _____

3. _____

4. _____

Descriptive Adjectives

> **A descriptive adjective describes a noun or a pronoun. It indicates a quality or condition of a noun.**
> <u>dark</u> coat, <u>clear</u> stream, <u>mild</u> cold

- Underline the descriptive adjective(s) in each of the following sentences.

  1. The dinosaurs were the dominant land animal 65 million years ago.

  2. The name was derived from a Greek word meaning "terrible lizard."

  3. These animals reached gigantic proportions.

  4. A large number of dinosaurs were flesh eaters.

  5. Some dinosaurs abandoned this diet for a herbivorous diet.

  6. The earlier and more primitive types were actually small, reptile-like animals.

  7. Suddenly the record of the huge monsters stops.

  8. How do we explain this sudden extinction?

  9. One theory blames temperature changes.

  10. Another theory suggests that geological changes occurred which reduced food sources.

  11. Many thrilling movies revolve around these amazing reptiles.

  12. Kids all over the world would miss hearing blood-curdling screams in their favorite dinosaur movies.

  13. Nervous children would not have to ask for their special night light.

  14. Brave parents wouldn't have to search the dark driveway for mysterious, scaly prowlers.

  15. Could you write an exciting book about these incredible creatures?

- Write five sentences about dinosaurs using at least one descriptive adjective in each. Underline the descriptive adjectives.

  1. _____

  2. _____

  3. _____

  4. _____

  5. _____

Comparative Degree of Adjectives

The comparative degree of an adjective is used when showing a comparison between two persons or things. It shows a greater or lesser degree of quality.

Almost every adjective of one syllable forms its comparative degree by adding *-er*.

>   stronger, neater, warmer

An adjective with two or more syllables forms its comparative degree by adding *more* or *less* in front of the adjective.

>   more clever, less difficult

An adjective that ends in *y* usually forms its comparative degree by changing the *y* to *i* and adding *-er*.

>   handier, clumsier

• In each of the following sentences, underline the adjective in the comparative degree.

1. It was a stormier night than usual at our cottage.

2. First there was a harder rain than we were used to seeing.

3. This was followed by stronger winds than we experience at home.

4. If the roof had been flimsier, it would have blown away.

5. But the roof was more sturdy than we thought.

6. I can't imagine a more dismal evening.

7. Large hailstones started to fall, followed by even larger ones.

8. My sister, who is younger than I am, was scared.

9. We heard a clap of thunder which was louder than an explosion.

10. The next day brought a calmer sky.

• Write four sentences of your own with each including at least one adjective in the comparative degree. Underline the comparative adjectives.

1. _____

2. _____

3. _____

4. _____

Superlative Degree of Adjectives

The superlative degree of an adjective is used when more than two persons or things are being compared. It indicates that the quality is possessed to the greatest or least degree by one of the persons or things being compared.

Adjectives of one syllable usually form the superlative degree by adding -est.

strongest, neatest, warmest

An adjective of two or more syllables forms the superlative degree by adding *most* or *least* in front of the adjective.

most clever, least difficult

An adjective that ends in *y* usually forms the superlative degree by changing the *y* to *i* and adding -est.

handiest, clumsiest

- In the following sentences, underline the adjectives that are in the superlative degree.

  1. That was the greatest movie I ever saw!

  2. It had the most glamorous stars in the most exotic settings imaginable.

  3. Even though the story was one of the tallest tales I've heard, I still enjoyed it.

  4. The hero had to perform the most difficult stunts of all.

  5. The special effects were the most intricate ever attempted.

  6. The part of the heroine was played by the most talented actress in the world.

  7. The villain was the nastiest character they could have found for the part.

  8. The weakest part of the film was the ending.

  9. It seems they selected the silliest conclusion possible.

- Write four sentences of your own about a movie you have seen. Each sentence should include at least one adjective in the superlative degree. Underline the superlative degree adjectives.

  1. _____

  2. _____

  3. _____

  4. _____

Irregular Comparison of Adjectives

Some adjectives have an irregular form of comparison. An irregular adjective forms the degree of comparison by a complete change in the word itself.

Note: Study the forms below before attempting the activity. Always consult a dictionary if you are in doubt about which form to use.

Positive	Comparative	Superlative
much	more	most
bad	worse	worst
good	better	best
far	farther	farthest
little	less	least

- In each of the following sentences, underline the irregular form of the adjective.

1. That was the best meal he has ever cooked.

2. He won a prize at the reunion because he drove a farther distance than anyone else.

3. Hank said he had a better day today than he had yesterday.

4. That is the worst poem I have ever read.

5. That is the most homework the class has ever been given.

6. The hungry girl ate less ham than eggs.

7. Of all the chefs, he added the least salt to his chili.

There are some adjectives that should not be compared because the positive degree is already the highest possible degree. For example, if something is *empty*, it cannot be *emptier*.

Examples: empty, correct, perfect, final, full, alone, wrong, supreme, single

- Use the following adjectives to write sentences of your own.

1. correct _____

2. final _____

3. perfect _____

Limiting Adjectives

A limiting adjective is one that points out an object or indicates its number or quantity. The articles *a, an,* and *the* are limiting adjectives. *A* precedes a noun beginning with a consonant sound, and *an* precedes a noun beginning with a vowel sound.

the cat, a dog, an owl, an hour

- Write **a** or **an** in front of each noun.

1. _____ garage	5. _____ ant	9. _____ honor	13. _____ car
2. _____ CD	6. _____ baseball	10. _____ sale	14. _____ uncle
3. _____ apple	7. _____ order	11. _____ elevator	15. _____ carpet
4. _____ disaster	8. _____ concert	12. _____ video	16. _____ floor

A numerical adjective is a limiting adjective that indicates an exact number.

one, thirty, fifty

- In the following sentences, circle the articles and underline the numerical adjectives.

1. The top speed limit on the interstate expressway is fifty-five miles per hour.

2. A two-hundred dollar fine may result if you speed.

3. There are only about five cars that pass this point every day.

4. Twenty police officers have been assigned to monitor the city streets.

5. If they save just one life, it will be worth the effort.

6. The traffic laws review book contained twenty-three pages.

7. I read the book ten times.

- Write sentences of your own about driving a car. Use a numerical adjective in each sentence.

1. _____

2. _____

3. _____

4. _____

5. _____

Demonstrative and Indefinite Adjectives

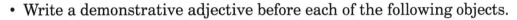

> ***This, that, these,*** and ***those*** are demonstrative adjectives
> that point out a particular person, place, or thing. Use
> ***this*** and ***these*** for things close by and ***that*** and ***those*** for
> things distant in time or space.

- Write a demonstrative adjective before each of the following objects.

  1. _____ tulips (near)   6. _____ umbrella (far)

  2. _____ boot (far)   7. _____ radio (far)

  3. _____ tables (near)   8. _____ stadium (near)

  4. _____ island (far)   9. _____ nation (far)

  5. _____ empires (far)   10. _____ textbooks (near)

- Choose the correct word or words for each sentence.

  1. (This, That) tree on the hill is beautiful.

  2. (These, Those) musicians playing now are more talented than (these, those) musicians we heard last week.

  3. (This, That) flower in my hand is more beautiful than the one in the vase.

  4. (This, That) apple you are holding looks shinier than (this, that) one right there.

> **An indefinite adjective is an adjective which gives an approximate number or
> quantity. It does not tell exactly how many or how much.**
> <u>many</u> mice, <u>more</u> choices, <u>fewer</u> decisions

- In the following sentences, circle the indefinite adjectives.

  1. Some politicians seemed to be making many promises.

  2. Few people could really understand what they wanted to do.

  3. Several reporters tried to pin them down to the facts.

  4. Many people in the crowd wanted an alternative.

  5. Finally more candidates came forward.

  6. They talked like they understood many problems.

  7. All people could support these candidates.

Proper and Interrogative Adjectives

A proper adjective is an adjective formed from a proper noun. It is always capitalized and may contain more than one word.
Latin American dances
Florida oranges

- Circle all the adjectives and write **P** above each proper adjective.

Italian sauce	new car	bright red apple	Irish stew
million years	Belgian waffles	other classes	Mexican border
Greek salad	California sunshine	Flag Day parade	Chicago museum
Siamese cat	few animals	United Nations building	French bread
several shoes	German dances	Swedish meatballs	silk shirt
Japanese food	purple book	African stories	English setter
small puppy	Michigan highway	orange balloon	digital clock

An interrogative adjective is an adjective which is used to ask a question.
what, which

- In each of the following sentences, circle the interrogative adjective and underline the noun it modifies.

1. Which part is missing from this computer?

2. What type of monitor do you have?

3. Which system works best for word processing?

4. What brand has the lowest price right now?

5. What store did you visit to look for a new computer?

- Write a short paragraph of your own about your neighborhood. Include two proper adjectives and two interrogative adjectives in the paragraph. Underline these adjectives.

_____

_____

_____

_____

   IF8732 Grammar 7–8

Predicate Adjectives

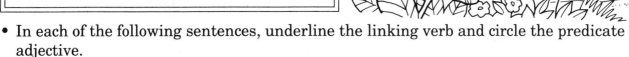

> **A predicate adjective follows a linking verb and describes the subject.**
> The fish was <u>fantastic</u>.

- In each of the following sentences, underline the linking verb and circle the predicate adjective.

  1. Bees are necessary for the process of pollination to be completed.

  2. Honey from the hives is delicious.

  3. The color is golden.

  4. Worker bees are very industrious.

  5. In the hierarchy of the hive, the queen bee is supreme.

  6. The eggs are tiny.

  7. Orchard owners are dependent on bees for their livelihood.

  8. They are happy to see the swarms of bees invade their trees.

  9. The mites which attack the hive are tiny.

  10. They are unpopular with everyone.

- Write a short paragraph of your own, using at least three predicate adjectives. Underline the predicate adjectives.

  _____

  _____

  _____

  _____

  _____

- Use the following linking verbs to write sentences of your own which include predicate adjectives.

  1. are _____

  2. were _____

  3. is _____

  4. was _____

Adverbs of Time

> An adverb is a word that modifies a verb, an adjective, or another adverb. Adverbs indicate time, place, or manner.
>
> Adverbs of time answer the question *when* or *how often*. They usually modify verbs.
>
> People <u>seldom</u> like to be given orders.

- In the following sentences, circle the adverbs of time and underline the verbs they modify.

1. People have always needed some form of government.

2. First came dictatorships of one form or another.

3. Then, the king or dictator made all of the decisions.

4. Eventually, the ancient Greeks established a form of government they called democracy.

5. It was called democracy, but the people who did not own land could never vote.

6. Later, the Romans adapted this system into a republican form of government.

7. Under this system, the results were often representative of the people's wishes.

8. This form was always better than the totalitarian forms which eventually followed.

9. Totalitarian governments frequently allow human rights abuses.

10. Today, people around the world look to the United States as a model of democracy.

11. They often feel that the democratic system works better than any other that has been tried before.

12. Even Americans are constantly working to improve their democratic system.

13. There is always room for improvement in any system.

- Use the following adverbs of time to write sentences of your own about a historical event you have studied recently. Underline the verbs that are being modified.

1. finally _____

2. seldom _____

3. already _____

4. frequently _____

5. often _____

6. usually _____

Adverbs of Place

> **Adverbs of place answer the question *where*.**
> **They usually modify verbs.**
>
> The fish swam <u>below</u>.

- In the following sentences, circle the adverbs of place and underline the verbs they modify.

   1. People have looked everywhere for a satisfactory type of government.

   2. The Japanese stayed away from the democratic style.

   3. They preferred a government system which developed nearby.

   4. Back in the mid 600s, an emperor ruled there.

   5. Sailors came here from Europe in 1543.

   6. Japan focused inward during the 1630s.

   7. In 1854, Commodore Perry brought in U.S. trade.

   8. By 1868, the emperor looked outside for ideas to modernize Japan.

   9. This technology spread out from the leaders to the people.

   10. Today, many Western nations look there for ways to improve their own economies.

- Write a short paragraph using three adverbs of place. Circle the adverbs of place and underline the verbs they modify.

   _____

   _____

   _____

   _____

   _____

- Use the following adverbs of place to write sentences of your own. Underline the verbs they modify.

   1. underneath _____

   2. away _____

   3. inside _____

   4. downward _____

Adverbs of Manner

> Adverbs of manner answer the question *how* or *in what manner.* They usually end in *-ly.*
>
> Do your work <u>thoroughly</u>.

- In the following sentences, circle the adverbs of manner and underline the verbs they modify.

1. People all over the world eagerly play association football, known here as soccer.

2. Beginners must listen carefully to understand the rules.

3. When they understand completely, they will be ready to play the game.

4. The round ball must be carefully controlled.

5. Soccer can easily be played almost anywhere.

6. It is exciting to watch players gracefully execute complex foot movements.

7. Fans react emotionally when their favorite team loses.

8. The game was first played competitively in Great Britain in the late 1800s.

9. Games like soccer were played passionately by the Chinese in the third century B.C.

10. Soccer spread rapidly from Great Britain throughout the world.

11. The World Cup, soccer's championship, is the most avidly watched soccer game in the world.

12. The United States has slowly begun to accept soccer.

13. Americans found out that it is a game that must be played intensely.

14. Someday, perhaps when the U.S. wins the World Cup, soccer will be taken seriously in this country.

15. Until then, U.S. fans will watch hopefully as other countries dominate the game.

- Write five sentences about a sport you like to play using an adverb of manner in each. Circle the adverbs of manner and underline the verbs that they modify.

1. _____

2. _____

3. _____

4. _____

5. _____

Comparison of Adverbs

Like adjectives, many adverbs also have degrees of comparison. The three degrees of comparison are positive, comparative, and superlative. Some adverbs form the comparative degree by adding *-er* and the superlative degree by adding *-est*. Most adverbs that end in *-ly* form their comparative degrees by adding the word *more* or *less* in front of the positive degree. The superlative degree is formed by adding the word *most* or *least* in front of the positive degree.

• Write the missing adverbs in the chart.

Positive	Comparative	Superlative
fast	faster	fastest
carefully	more/less carefully	most/least carefully
soon		
hard		
noisily		
late		
easily		
efficiently		
loudly		
proudly		
harshly		
neatly		
cheerfully		
courageously		
highly		

• In the following sentences circle the adverbs and indicate the degree of comparison. (**P**—positive, **C**—comparative, **S**—superlative)

_____ 1. In order to be a good goalie, you have to react more quickly than the average person.

_____ 2. The puck slides across the ice fast.

_____ 3. The teammate skating nearest will help you fend off the attack.

_____ 4. You might be pushed roughly onto the ice.

_____ 5. When a player has the puck, watch him or her more carefully.

_____ 6. The player who guides the puck most skillfully makes many goals.

_____ 7. A good player is less easily discouraged than you would think.

_____ 8. That player gets back on the ice most quickly.

Adverbs and Adjectives

> When trying to determine whether to use an adjective or
> an adverb, decide which word is being modified.
> Adjectives modify nouns and pronouns. Adverbs modify
> verbs, adjectives, and other adverbs.

- In the following sentences, circle the correct word. Then identify it by writing **ADV** (adverb)
  or **ADJ** (adjective) in the blank.

_____ 1. The sound track began very (strange, strangely).

_____ 2. There was a (sudden, suddenly) surge of volume.

_____ 3. This was followed by an announcer (calm, calmly) announcing the names of the cast.

_____ 4. It is not the (usual, usually) way for a film to begin.

_____ 5. The credits were (extreme, extremely) long.

_____ 6. We were (true, truly) in for a different experience.

_____ 7. (Gradual, Gradually) the actual movie started.

_____ 8. I had been (wise, wisely) to go out for popcorn during the credits.

_____ 9. But I felt (guilty, guiltily) because I didn't bring my sister any.

_____10. The plot moved (swift, swiftly) into a series of wild chases.

_____11. Each one was performed more (awkward, awkwardly) than the last.

_____12. The actors' performances were very (poor, poorly).

_____13. I can't remember when I saw a more (odd, oddly) movie.

_____14. I couldn't get out of there (quick, quickly) enough.

_____15. Next time, I'm going to read the review more (thorough, thoroughly).

- Use the following adjectives and adverbs in sentences of your own. Circle the modifiers and
  underline the words being modified.

1. clever _____

2. gradually _____

3. honest _____

4. genuinely _____

5. happily _____

6. great _____

Double Negatives

> **A double negative is an incorrect construction that uses two negative words when one is sufficient. Use only one negative word when you mean "no."**
> Incorrect: He did <u>not</u> do <u>nothing</u> all day. (two negative words)
> Correct: He did <u>not</u> do anything all day. (or) He did <u>nothing</u> all day. (one negative word)

- Circle the negative words in the following sentences. Then rewrite each sentence so that it does not contain a double negative construction.

1. I haven't got no time to wait for you.

   _____

2. You don't know nothing about the subject we're discussing.

   _____

3. You can't hardly find that tape anywhere.

   _____

4. Oprah said that she didn't want no one on the show with his attitude.

   _____

5. David couldn't hardly believe his good luck.

   _____

6. My brother doesn't do nothing all day long.

   _____

7. Gerald hasn't never been to New York City before.

   _____

8. The police told the press that they would not have no further statements until Monday.

   _____

9. Polly didn't have nowhere to go, so she pouted.

   _____

10. All of this work doesn't scarcely leave time for me to play.

   _____

- Use the negative words below to write sentences of your own about safety rules.

   1. never _____

   2. nothing _____

   3. could not _____

   4. no _____

   5. have not _____

Adjective Prepositional Phrases

A prepositional phrase is a group of words that shows how two words or ideas are related to each other. It can function as an adjective or an adverb depending on the word it modifies. Like a one-word adjective, an adjective prepositional phrase modifies a noun or pronoun.

The shady ground <u>under the elm tree</u> was perfect.

- In the following sentences, underline the prepositional phrases and circle the words being modified.

1. People in the news are frequently embarrassed.

2. The drugstore in town is open today.

3. The musical with the best choreography will win.

4. A gorilla in a red jumpsuit and a chimpanzee in a chiffon dress ran into the tent.

5. The cottage beside the gurgling brook was sold a year ago.

6. The list of students' addresses was burned in the fire this morning.

7. Nobody in this class knows.

8. The doctors in this hospital are working very hard.

9. The combination to the safe is lost.

10. The CD on the computer is amazing.

- Write your own sentences using the prepositional phrases below as adjectives. Underline the phrase and circle the preposition.

1. for the defense _____

2. beside the lake _____

3. below the green umbrella _____

4. above the slimy seaweed _____

5. amid the thick fog _____

6. with the red flag _____

7. on the sailboat _____

Adverb Prepositional Phrases

> Like a one-word adverb, an adverb prepositional phrase usually modifies a verb and may tell *where, how,* or *when* an action takes place.
>
> We play ball <u>in the park</u>. (Tells *where* we *play*)
>
> She called <u>in a loud voice</u>. (Tells *how* she *called*)
>
> Mom gave us smiles <u>throughout the day</u>. (Tells *when* Mom *gave*)

- In the following sentences, underline the prepositional phrases and circle the words being modified.

1. The stands sagged under the students' weight.

2. My biology book fell into the puddle.

3. Ron, the champion runner, jumped over the hurdle with ease.

4. The gifts were wrapped with care and placed under the tree.

5. Marithia and Tinita walked under the bridge.

6. Several jumpers pushed from the plane too early.

7. The firefighters rushed into the forest.

8. After the defeat the team traveled alone through the night.

9. You will find Gerald sitting behind the barn.

10. The Amish travel everywhere in their buggies.

11. The birds flew into the tree.

12. The girl danced with graceful movements.

13. Lightning flashes around the clouds.

14. A tornado moves with shocking speed.

- Write your own sentences using the prepositional phrases below as adverbs. Underline the phrase and circle the preposition.

1. in another language _____

2. in his math class _____

3. under the bed _____

4. during the fifth inning _____

Interjections

> **Interjections are words that express strong feeling or sudden emotion. They may be followed by an exclamation point or a comma. Interjections are more effective when they are not overused.**
>
> Hey! Look at that hawk. <u>Oh</u>, that's a surprise.

- Underline the interjections in the following sentences.

  1. Wow! It's my birthday today!

  2. Great! I can't wait for my friends to get here.

  3. No! What do you mean they can't come?

  4. Oh no! This is terrible!

  5. Oh, quit complaining.

  6. Rats! I thought this was going to be a great day.

  7. Zounds! I have an idea!

  8. Shh, listen.

  9. Yes! This just might work.

  10. Right! I'll call some of my other friends and see if they can come.

  11. Ah, I love that idea.

  12. Hey! Did you hear that?

  13. Surprise! We came after all!

  14. Gosh! I sure was worried for a while.

  15. Super! It was a great celebration!

- Use the interjections given here to write sentences of your own.

  1. Hey _____

  2. Wow _____

  3. Alas _____

  4. Stop _____

  5. Ouch _____

- Write two sentences describing a ride at an amusement park. Include an interjection in each sentence.

  1. _____

  2. _____

Conjunctions

> **A conjunction is a word that joins words or groups of words together. There are three types of conjunctions: coordinating, correlative, and subordinating.**
> **Coordinating conjunctions:** and, but, or, nor, for, yet, so
> **Correlative conjunctions:** either—or, both—and, whether—or, neither—nor, not only—but also (These are always used in pairs.)
> **Some common subordinating conjunctions:** after, although, as, as if, because, before, if, since, that, though, until, when, while

• In the following sentences, circle the conjunctions. Identify what kind of conjunction each is by writing letters in the blanks: **CO**—coordinating, **CR**—correlative, **SU**—subordinating.

____ 1. Moscow is Russia's largest city and its political capital as well.

____ 2. It is also a commercial, cultural, and communications center.

____ 3. It is known as a center for heavy machinery manufacturing, but it has other important industries.

____ 4. Neither the czars nor the communist dictators were able to take the heart from Moscow's people.

____ 5. We will understand the people of Moscow if we study their history.

____ 6. Some of that history was hidden, though it is now coming to light.

____ 7. Though Moscow remained an important center of culture and trade, St. Petersburg became the new capital.

____ 8. Moscow was somewhat weakened because every effort was made to make St. Petersburg the center of attention.

____ 9. This was encouraged for two centuries but was stopped in 1917 with the Russian Revolution.

____ 10. The capital was once again Moscow when the government fell to the Bolsheviks.

____ 11. Moscow grew rapidly in the 1930s, and the city gained power.

____ 12. During World War II, Germans not only used planes to bomb the city but also approached the city with foot soldiers.

• Write three sentences about your country, using a conjunction in each. Underline the conjunction.

1. _____

2. _____

3. _____

Same Word—Different Part of Speech

There are many words whose function as a part of
speech varies depending on how they are used in a
particular sentence.

The answer was <u>right</u>. (an adjective)

What <u>right</u> do you have to say that? (a noun)

I will <u>right</u> all of the wrongs committed. (a verb)

- Identify the part of speech of each boldfaced word: adjective,
  adverb, noun, pronoun, verb, or preposition.

_____ 1. He slid **down** head first.

_____ 2. Did you notice an unusual **smell** when you walked in?

_____ 3. **Some** are planning to visit the art museum while others are
                     intending to go out for lunch.

_____ 4. The people of this **country** want real leadership.

_____ 5. The itsy-bitsy spider slid **down** the water spout.

_____ 6. I **smell** a rat!

_____ 7. Doris signed up for a class in **country** painting.

_____ 8. **Some** people really enjoyed the dance we went to last night.

_____ 9. Terri said that it was the most moving **play** she had ever seen.

_____ 10. Hannah **played** with her little sister while I fixed dinner.

- Write your own sentences using the following words as the specified parts of speech
  given below.

1. <u>musical</u> (noun) _____

2. <u>safe</u> (adjective) _____

3. <u>work</u> (verb) _____

4. <u>train</u> (noun) _____

5. <u>musical</u> (adjective) _____

6. <u>safe</u> (noun) _____

7. <u>work</u> (noun) _____

8. <u>train</u> (verb) _____

Identifying Parts of Speech—Review

Noun—names a person, place, thing, or idea
Pronoun—takes the place of a noun
Verb—shows action or state of being
Adjective—modifies a noun or pronoun
Adverb—modifies a verb, adjective, or
     another adverb
	Preposition—relates a noun or pronoun to
	     another word
	Conjunction—links words or groups of words
	Interjection—expresses strong emotion or
	     surprise

• In each of the following sentences, identify the part of speech of the underlined word.

_____ 1. A city must be planned <u>carefully</u>, or people will not want to live in it.

_____ 2. We were going to attend the game, but the meteorologist <u>predicted</u> rain.

_____ 3. I am going to do <u>my</u> homework after school, but I would rather play with my friends.

_____ 4. Sheila put a <u>dollar</u> into the pop machine, but nothing came out.

_____ 5. Doris skidded <u>around</u> the corner, and she lost control of the car.

_____ 6. The paperboy drove <u>past</u>, and he threw the paper into the bushes.

_____ 7. Wash the car <u>and</u> wax it.

_____ 8. My mother and I went to two movies and liked <u>both</u> of them.

_____ 9. How will you <u>pay</u> for this damage, and when can I expect the money?

_____ 10. Gloria will examine the car, <u>though</u> Ted will buy it.

_____ 11. The catfish swam near <u>the</u> surface, and the cat tried to snag him.

_____ 12. The team won the game, and the crowd <u>waited</u> outside the stadium to cheer them.

_____ 13. A fee must be paid, or you will not be allowed to use this <u>facility</u>.

_____ 14. Either the test was <u>very</u> difficult, or those students are not studying hard enough.

_____ 15. The Trojan War was made <u>famous</u> in Homer's *Iliad*.

_____ 16. Vancouver is a <u>popular</u> tourist destination.

_____ 17. The Biblical name for <u>Israel</u> and surrounding land was Canaan.

_____ 18. The Arthurian legends tell the <u>tale</u> of King Arthur and his Knights of the Round Table.

_____ 19. The Battle of Manila Bay was fought <u>during</u> the Spanish- American War.

_____ 20. <u>Wow</u>! Trent is going to visit the new museum.

Participles and Participial Phrases

A participle is a verb form that functions as an adjective. A participial phrase is a group of words that includes the participle and its related words.

The present participle is usually formed by adding *-ing* to the present tense verb.
Participle: The runner enjoyed the <u>cooling</u> breezes.
Participial phrase: <u>Cooling off</u>, the runners jumped into the pool.

The past participle is usually formed by adding *-ed* to the present tense. Check your dictionary for the way irregular verbs form the past participle.
Participle: Each <u>sunburned</u> person would be uncomfortable tonight.
Participial phrase: <u>Burned by the sun</u>, the teenager reached for a t-shirt.

- In each of the following sentences, underline the participle and circle the word that it modifies.

  1. We tiptoed around the sleeping child.

  2. The surging river terrified the townspeople.

  3. Each contestant auditioned her singing voice for the pageant.

  4. The dried flowers were carefully hung in the barn.

  5. The satisfied customers left the restaurant determined to come back.

  6. The city removed the wrecked cars.

  7. A watched pot never boils.

  8. You could tell he was scared because of his shaking knees.

  9. A startling rumor spread quickly through the school.

  10. Jane owns a flourishing business.

- In each of the following sentences, underline the participial phrase and circle the word that it modifies.

  1. Opening the door, Greg saw a huge crowd of people.

  2. The car pictured in the brochure was a Chevy.

  3. Donald saw a giraffe eating leaves.

  4. Breathing hard, the runner collapsed.

  5. The police, knocking loudly on the door, awakened everybody.

  6. Entering the store, Frieda walked down the center aisle.

  7. Slipping into the water, the diver disappeared.

  8. Walking quickly, Ron soon reached the depot.

Gerunds and Gerund Phrases

A gerund is a verb form ending in *-ing* that functions as a noun. Gerunds are formed by adding *-ing* to the present tense verb form.

<u>Painting</u> is my favorite hobby.

A gerund phrase is a group of words that includes a gerund and its related words.

<u>Painting the ceiling</u> is a difficult job.

• In each of the following sentences, underline the gerund and indicate how it is being used in the sentence: subject (**S,**) direct object (**DO**), object of preposition (**OP**), or predicate noun (**PN**).

_____ 1. Exercising is the best thing you can do for yourself.

_____ 2. My favorite hobby is skiing.

_____ 3. Don enjoys painting.

_____ 4. Sarah likes skating.

_____ 5. The tolling of the bells is getting on my nerves.

_____ 6. Whispering is not polite.

_____ 7. You can become a pro by practicing.

_____ 8. Jogging has become a very popular activity.

_____ 9. Whenever I go to a swim meet, I enjoy the diving most.

• In the following sentences, underline the gerund phrase and indicate its use in the sentence (**S, DO, OP, PN**).

_____ 1. Susan was soon bored with reading her book.

_____ 2. Teresa enjoys reading historical novels.

_____ 3. Flipping hamburgers is a good way to make some money.

_____ 4. The referee began by introducing the players to one another.

_____ 5. Drinking a lot of water is good for you.

_____ 6. Ron's new task is collecting newspapers to recycle.

_____ 7. Asking questions is probably the best way to learn something.

_____ 8. Playing baseball is my idea of an enjoyable afternoon.

_____ 9. Measuring the ingredients in the recipe will ensure good results.

_____10. She passed her opponent by running faster.

_____11. His goal was playing chess in the world championship.

Infinitives and Infinitive Phrases

> **An infinitive is a present tense verb and is usually preceded by *to*. It is often used as a noun serving as a subject, a direct object, or a predicate noun.**
>
> To win the race is her goal. (subject)
> She hopes to win. (direct object)
> Ellen's goal is to win the race. (predicate noun)

- In each of the following sentences, underline the infinitive. Indicate if the infinitive is used as a subject (**S**), a direct object (**DO**), or predicate noun (**PN**).

_____ 1. On a snowy day I like to ski.

_____ 2. To fish is all my grandpa ever wanted out of life.

_____ 3. My father was hoping to play.

_____ 4. Would you like to go?

_____ 5. To debate is the reason that we are gathered here.

_____ 6. To sleep was my only thought.

_____ 7. One sacred responsibility is to vote.

_____ 8. I did not dare to speak.

_____ 9. The purpose of talking is to communicate.

- In each of the following sentences, underline the infinitive phrase which is used as a noun and indicate whether it is a subject (**S**), a direct object (**DO**), or predicate noun (**PN**).

_____ 1. The club's goal was to raise one thousand dollars.

_____ 2. Gilda expected to pass the class with ease.

_____ 3. Seth decided to go to the game by himself.

_____ 4. To finish this paper by tomorrow will be very difficult.

_____ 5. He did not dare to make the trip alone.

_____ 6. To win a championship must be very exciting.

_____ 7. Several people helped to rescue the boy.

_____ 8. The teacher tried to show us several ways of solving the problem.

_____ 9. Dorothy wanted to have it all.

_____ 10. To swing from a rope over the river can be challenging.

_____ 11. Those books need to be saved.

_____ 12. Chris planned to run for president of his class.

_____ 13. The hungry workers hoped to get a good meal.

More Verbals

Name _____

> **Verbals—participles, gerunds, and infinitives—are verb forms that do not perform as verbs. Instead, they function as other parts of speech.**

• In each of the following sentences, underline the verbal phrase and indicate whether it is a participial phrase (**P**), a gerund phrase (**G**), or an infinitive phrase (**I**).

_____ 1. He was asked to buy some fresh vegetables.

_____ 2. Known as one of the best pitchers in baseball, Warren Spahn was inducted into the Hall of Fame.

_____ 3. Kelly practices juggling three apples at a time.

_____ 4. Lexi tried to study on a regular basis.

_____ 5. It is important to exercise every day.

_____ 6. Talking to himself, my brother walked down the street.

_____ 7. Reggie volunteered to have everybody over for dinner.

_____ 8. Taking a vitamin is the way he starts his day.

_____ 9. Standing up to his knees in the water, Wes cast his fly into the river.

_____ 10. The boys all want to go to the amusement park.

_____ 11. Exhausted from the long journey, the fish wallowed in the shallow water.

_____ 12. Hooking rugs is a very interesting hobby for many.

_____ 13. The principal, depressed by the poor attendance, worked on a new plan.

_____ 14. Baking cookies helps relieve my tension.

_____ 15. Anne likes painting seashells.

• Write your own sentences including the indicated verb forms.

1. (participial) _____

2. (participial) _____

3. (gerund) _____

4. (gerund) _____

5. (infinitive) _____

6. (infinitive) _____

Misplaced and Dangling Modifiers

Modifiers that are not placed near the words or phrases that they modify are called misplaced modifiers.

Misplaced modifier: <u>Chilled to the bone</u>, the hot soup tasted good to the skiers.

(Here *chilled to the bone* modifies the word *skiers* but is not placed near it.)

- Underline the misplaced modifiers and then write the sentences correctly.

1. The women's group is offering counseling for those who need it on Monday.

   _____

2. The new car was very popular with the race fans which raced past.

   _____

3. The company decided to buy a new building which needed more space.

   _____

4. The number increases every year of boating accidents.

   _____

5. There is a special item in that store that is on sale today.

   _____

If a modifying word, phrase, or clause does not modify a particular word, then the modifier is called a dangling modifier. Every modifier must have a word that it clearly modifies.

Incorrect: <u>Entering the bay</u>, the city loomed in front of us.
(*Entering the bay* does not modify *city*)

Correct: <u>Entering the bay</u>, the boat began to head toward shore.
(*Entering the bay* correctly modifies *the boat*)

- In the following sentences, underline the dangling modifiers. If the modifier is used correctly, write **OK** in the blank.

_____ 1. Chilled by the snow, it felt good to be inside.

_____ 2. In the summer catalog, the models looked elegant.

_____ 3. Living on the beach all summer, the sun-block supply was quite low.

_____ 4. Startled by the wild animal, the scream caused me to whirl around suddenly.

_____ 5. Living in the woods, the trapper was a contented man.

_____ 6. Humbled by the speech, the look that was given said it all.

_____ 7. After it had been scraped, the toast tasted fine.

Independent and Dependent Clauses

> **An independent clause is a group of words with a subject and a predicate that expresses a complete thought and can stand by itself as a sentence.**
>
> <u>Jack played golf</u> until it was too dark to see.
> (Independent clause)
>
> **A dependent clause cannot stand alone. It depends upon the independent clause of the sentence to complete its meaning. Dependent clauses start with words like** *who, which, that, because, when, if, until, before,* **and** *after.*
>
> <u>If the people support Hank</u>, he will run.
> (Dependent clause)

- In each of the following sentences, underline the independent clause once and the dependent clause twice.

1. When the cold weather arrives, I'm going south.

2. The whole class really enjoyed the movie that showed life under the sea.

3. If you think you know the answer, raise your hand.

4. I was about to leave for my vacation when I noticed that the tire was flat.

5. Fred really liked the car that we bought for him at the auction.

6. Theresa was really disappointed that we could not go.

7. Until history became Henry's favorite subject, it was not easy for him to get a good grade.

8. When David builds a new radio-controlled car, we're going to race each other.

9. The cottage which we had purchased was old and dilapidated.

10. If the pain does not go away, please call the doctor.

11. Sheila knows many people who can play bridge.

12. Ted thought he knew just how she felt because he'd had the same experience.

13. I have not yet heard the song that the popular singer recorded in Finnish.

14. The paramedics grabbed the oxygen when they saw the patient turning blue.

15. You have not lived until you take a trip down the Colorado River in a raft.

16. When I returned to the store, he had already left.

17. She wants a new truck that will handle well on rough terrain.

Adjective Clauses

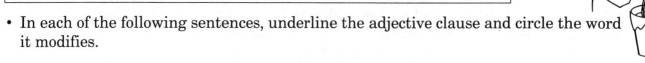

An adjective clause is a dependent clause that functions as an adjective. It can modify any noun or pronoun in a sentence.

The politician <u>who won the election</u> saluted his supporters.

- In each of the following sentences, underline the adjective clause and circle the word it modifies.

1. Shawn knows the teacher who gave you the detention.

2. Traditions that seem to have disappeared often return.

3. The painter tried to match the color that was used before.

4. The activity that Gentry most enjoyed was diving from the falls.

5. I bought the desk that was in the front window.

6. He put his hand under the table that had been freshly painted.

7. Sally is the person who applied for the job.

8. The police officer whose gun fell from his holster was very embarrassed.

9. The lake where they caught all of the fish was far away.

10. The city which we visited was one of the cleanest in the state.

11. The play to which the critic referred was a bomb.

12. The horse that I bet on fell during the race.

13. You will have to tell me the names of the students who might help us.

14. A wall that faces south will absorb a lot of solar heat.

- Write five sentences about your neighborhood. Include an adjective clause in each. Underline each adjective clause and circle the noun or pronoun modified.

1. _____

2. _____

3. _____

4. _____

5. _____

Adverb Clauses

> **An adverb clause is a dependent clause that functions as an adverb. It can modify a verb, an adjective, or another adverb. Adverb clauses tell *how, when, where,* or *why* an action happened.**
>
> We ate <u>when Grandpa arrived</u>. (modifies *ate*; tells *when*)

• In each of the following sentences, underline the adverb clause and write the question it answers: **how, when, where,** or **why**.

_____ 1. You should listen carefully when the teacher speaks.

_____ 2. Since I read the book, I disliked the movie.

_____ 3. The doctor was very nervous before he began the surgery.

_____ 4. Everything began when Jed entered the room.

_____ 5. Ellen's reading will be the last because it is the best.

_____ 6. Because you have been so nice, I will allow you to move ahead of me.

_____ 7. Before Julie started running, she felt tired all the time.

_____ 8. He looked where the backpack was last seen.

_____ 9. I can stay afloat by moving my arms.

_____ 10. After the class is over, I will tell you a secret about the professor.

_____ 11. When you get to the light, turn left.

_____ 12. She practiced every day because she wanted to join the team.

_____ 13. Since the book was about Hawaii, I found it interesting.

_____ 14. Ken visited his mother whenever he could.

_____ 15. Before the practice began, the coach gave a short pep talk.

• Write five sentences about a hobby you enjoy. For each sentence, include an adverb clause which answers the indicated question.

1. (how) _____

2. (when) _____

3. (where) _____

4. (why) _____

Noun Clauses

A noun clause is a dependent clause that functions as a noun. It may be used as a subject, a direct object, an indirect object, an object of a preposition, or a predicate noun.

    <u>What happened</u> surprised everyone. (subject)

    George wondered <u>what he could do</u>. (direct object)

    Alyson will give <u>whoever wants one</u> a cookie. (indirect object)

    The children did not laugh until <u>the end of the play</u>. (object of preposition)

    The problem is <u>what we will eat when we get there</u>. (predicate noun)

- In each of the following sentences, underline the noun clause and indicate how the clause is used in the sentence—subject (**S**), direct object (**DO**), indirect object (**IO**), object of a preposition (**OP**), or predicate noun (**PN**).

_____ 1. That you should eat your vegetables is certainly true.

_____ 2. What Heather did today was very difficult.

_____ 3. The meteorologists agreed that rain was expected.

_____ 4. The bus will depart at whatever time you designate.

_____ 5. A good movie is what I would like to see today.

_____ 6. I will give whoever comes to the door the message.

_____ 7. Whose books these are is obvious.

_____ 8. This prize will be awarded to whoever completes the course.

_____ 9. Life is what you make it.

_____ 10. What you say is not the truth.

_____ 11. How a computer works is a mystery to me.

_____ 12. Whoever wrote this graffiti will be punished.

_____ 13. A chance at the big time was what the minor league players craved.

_____ 14. I know that this plan will work.

- Write five sentences of your own, each of which includes a noun clause used as indicated.

1. (direct object) _____

2. (subject) _____

3. (predicate noun) _____

4. (object of a preposition) _____

5. (indirect object) _____

Identifying Clauses

An adjective clause is a dependent clause that functions as an adjective modifying nouns or pronouns.

An adverb clause is a dependent clause that functions as an adverb modifying verbs, adjectives, or other adverbs.

A noun clause is a dependent clause that functions as a noun.

- In each of the following sentences, underline the dependent clause and indicate if it is an adjective clause (**ADJ**), an adverb clause (**ADV**), or a noun clause (**N**).

_____ 1. Davis read the pamphlet to whoever would listen.

_____ 2. How you play the game is important.

_____ 3. Green is a color that is considered soothing.

_____ 4. I would like you to wait so that we can go together.

_____ 5. We already know what his real problem is.

_____ 6. The tornado that hit the town destroyed many homes.

_____ 7. Greg eats hotdogs when he is at the ball park.

_____ 8. Ralph played until he could barely move.

_____ 9. The director denied that he had stolen the idea for the movie.

_____ 10. Lake Superior, which is one of the Great Lakes, is the largest of the five.

_____ 11. The really bad news was that we couldn't go to the play.

_____ 12. The painting that we lost is worth a lot of money.

_____ 13. When the fish jumped out of the water, we realized that it was huge.

- Add an independent clause to each of the dependent clauses below to make a complete sentence.

1. **who fell from the tree** (adjective clause)

   _____

2. **that her dress was beautiful** (noun clause)

   _____

3. **when the river rises above this point** (adverb clause)

   _____

Punctuating Direct Quotations

> **Quotation marks are used to enclose direct quotations. The end punctuation usually comes before the final quotation mark at the end of the quote.**
>
>   Mary said, "Where are we going?"
>
> **Always capitalize the first word of a direct quotation. Do not capitalize the first word in the second part of an interrupted quote unless the second part begins a new sentence.**
>
>   "When it starts to snow," he said, "put on your heavy coat."
>
>   "Where did he go?" asked Bob. "We need him."

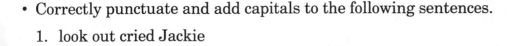

- Correctly punctuate and add capitals to the following sentences.

  1. look out cried Jackie

     _____

  2. didn't you see that broken step Jackie asked

     _____

  3. no said Anne thanks for warning me

     _____

  4. i think we should fix that before someone gets hurt Jackie suggested

     _____

  5. do you know where there's a hammer Ann queried

     _____

  6. i don't admitted Jackie but maybe Emily does

     _____

  7. hey Emily she yelled where's the hammer

     _____

  8. don't yell responded Emily i'm right behind you

     _____

- Write three sentences with direct quotations below. Include at least one interrogative and one exclamatory quotation.

  1. _____

  2. _____

  3. _____

Direct/Indirect Quotations

> **A direct quotation is the use of someone's exact words. It is always set off with quotation marks.**
>
> Kati said, "I am going to the beach today."
>
> **An indirect quotation is the writer's description of someone else's words. It does not require quotation marks.**
>
> Dave said that Kati was going to the beach today.

- For each of the following sentences, write **DQ** (direct quotation) or **IQ** (indirect quotation) in the blank. Then add quotation marks wherever they are needed.

_____ 1. Phoebe said, We're going to the Winter Olympics!

_____ 2. How are you getting there? asked Jaime.

_____ 3. At the same time, Della asked Phoebe what her favorite event was.

_____ 4. We're flying, said Phoebe, and I can't wait to go!

_____ 5. Jeff said that he'd never flown in an airplane.

_____ 6. Phoebe then said her favorite event is figure skating.

_____ 7. Are you really going to see the figure skating? asked Anne.

_____ 8. Phoebe said, Yes, my father has already bought tickets.

_____ 9. Well, I'd rather see the downhill skiing, interjected Jaime.

_____ 10. Anne said that she would rather see something beautiful and not have to worry about people getting hurt.

_____ 11. Della said she understood what Anne was talking about.

_____ 12. May I come along with you? implored Della.

- Write two sentences that contain direct quotations and two sentences that contain indirect quotations.

1. (direct) _____

2. (direct) _____

3. (indirect) _____

4. (indirect) _____

Other Uses for Quotation Marks

Single quotation marks are used to set off a quotation within a quotation.

"When did you tell me, 'I'm going with you'?" asked Dad.

The commercial asked, "How do you spell 'relief'?"

Quotation marks are used to set off words, phrases, or sentences referred to within a sentence.

You spell relief "r-e-l-i-e-f."

Quotation marks are used to set off slang words and expressions.

The pitcher threw the hitter a "spitter."

Quotation marks are used to set off the titles of magazine articles, names of songs, titles of poems, and chapters of books.

The magazine always includes a section entitled "Letters to the Editor."

• Add quotation marks as needed to the sentences below.

1. Chicago is my favorite poem, said Bill.

2. That's just because you grew up there, replied Rickie.

3. That's not true, corrected Bill. I like the way Sandburg writes.

4. When Bill said, I like the way Sandburg writes, I think he really meant it, added Hillary.

5. Did you do your homework yet? asked Bob.

6. I read the chapter Westward Bound in my history book, said Georgia.

7. Georgia started singing Home on the Range.

8. The class read The Gift of the Magi.

9. Sara wondered if The Furnished Room was included in that book of short stories.

10. The term short story is defined in the glossary.

11. George wondered what authors the teacher considered flaky.

12. What kind of question is that? the teacher asked.

13. Is that word in the dictionary? inquired Alex.

14. Did George say, I'll look that up? inquired the teacher.

Comma Use

A comma is used to set off an introductory phrase or dependent clause.

When you get home, we'll go to the mall.

A comma is used after words of direct address at the beginning of the sentence.

Michael, call me when you get home.

A comma is used after introductory words such as *yes, indeed, well, in addition, thus*, and *moreover*.

Yes, I agree with you completely.

Thus, the game ended before it had begun.

Use two commas to set off interrupting words or expressions.

Have you, by the way, ordered lunch yet?

• Add commas to the following sentences.

1. When I graduate from high school I plan to go to college.

2. Yes that is a good idea.

3. Of course you will need good grades to get into the college of your choice.

4. Seeing that you are a good student I know you'll have no problem.

5. In addition your involvement in extracurricular activities is important.

6. Ted what will you be studying in college?

7. If I get there I'd like to study oceanography.

8. Well you will have your work cut out for you.

9. You will find I'm sure that it is a competitive field.

10. Indeed it won't be easy.

11. Jack how about you?

12. I would like I think to go to medical school.

13. Fortunately I've been studying hard all year.

• Write three sentences, each having a correctly punctuated introductory element.

1. _____

2. _____

3. _____

     IF8732 Grammar 7–8

Capitalization

> **The words *north, south, east,* and *west* are not capitalized when they refer to directions. They are capitalized when they refer to specific sections of the country.**
>
>   Henry traveled <u>east</u> to see his sister.
>   Henry traveled to the <u>East Coast</u> to see his mother.
>
> **The names given to planets and stars are capitalized, but words like planet, sun, moon, and star are not capitalized.**
>
>   The pieces of the comet bombarded <u>Jupiter</u>.
>   The <u>moon</u> rose in the night sky.
>
> **The words derived from proper nouns are usually capitalized.**
>
>   The <u>American</u> tourists started snapping pictures.
>
> **Names of deities and sacred books are capitalized.**
>
>   <u>Jehovah</u>, the <u>*Koran*</u>

• In each of the following sentences, circle the words that should be capitalized.

1. we live east of the river.

2. living in the midwest gives one a different view of the world.

3. the two scientists disagreed about the impact of the comet.

4. if you drive far enough north, you will avoid the traffic jams.

5. yolanda likes to watch the latin american dances.

7. some people had a hard time realizing that the south had lost the war.

8. there is a passage in the bible which talks about forgiveness.

9. the boy studied the talmud.

• Use the words below to write sentences of your own which are correctly punctuated and capitalized.

1. german _____

2. elizabethan theater _____

3. venus _____

4. the mideast _____

5. the south _____

More Capitalization

Capitalize special titles when they precede a person's name.

You would never guess that <u>Doctor</u> Gregory is a brain surgeon.

Capitalize geographic names.

Our family made the drive up <u>Pikes Peak</u>.

Capitalize the names of streets, bridges, dams, hotels, monuments, parks, etc.

My brother was in a demonstration in <u>Grant Park</u>.

Capitalize the names of historical periods, historical events, and historical documents.

We just finished studying the <u>French Revolution</u>.

Capitalize the names of government bodies and departments.

The <u>Food and Drug Administration</u> approved the new serum for public use.

• Circle the words that need capitals.

1. Have you ever sailed on lake michigan?

2. The battle of midway was a turning point in world war II.

3. The bill sponsored by senator javits was defeated.

4. The plaza hotel in new york city is one of the most famous hotels in the world.

5. He was elected to the house of representatives.

6. The senators walked toward the white house.

7. Maybe we could get that information from the library of congress.

• Use the words below to write sentences of your own which are correctly punctuated and capitalized.

1. president washington

_____

2. the u.s. postal service

_____

3. san francisco bay

_____

4. the battle of gettysburg

_____

And More Capitalization

Capitalize the main words in the titles of books, movies, magazines, songs, etc. Do not capitalize prepositions, coordinate conjunctions, or articles unless they are the first or last words of the title.

> _Pride and Prejudice_ is my favorite book.

Do not capitalize the names of school subjects unless they are languages or unless they are followed by a number indicating a specific course.

> Wally is taking <u>English</u> and biology this term.

> All freshmen must take <u>Algebra 101</u>.

Capitalize words that show family relationship when they are used instead of a name or as part of a name.

> My <u>Uncle Don</u> has the greatest sense of humor.

> Does your uncle have a sense of humor?

• Circle the words which should be capitalized.

my mom	aunt sarah	<u>good housekeeping</u>
grandmothers	grandma	"the drummer boy of shiloh"
english	history	<u>the american heritage dictionary</u>
chemistry 101	your cousin	"stopping by woods on a snowy evening"
dad	uncle john	"born in the u.s.a."

• Use the following words to write sentences of your own which are correctly punctuated and capitalized.

1. aunt gertrude _____

2. cousin _____

3. french _____

4. america the beautiful _____

5. u.s. news and world report _____

6. biology 344 _____

7. the great gatsby _____

8. geometry _____

9. my father _____

10. national geographic _____

Problem Pairs

> There are certain pairs of words which are frequently confused; some sound alike, some are spelled similarly, and some have similar meanings.
>
> **already** – previously; **all ready** – all prepared
> **altogether** – entirely; **all together** – everyone in one group or place
> **its** – possessive form of it; **it's** – contraction of "it is"
> **there** – at that place; **their** – possessive form of they; **they're** –
>   contraction of "they are"
> **than** – conjunction used in comparisons; **then** – at that time
> **who's** – contraction of "who is" or "who has"; **whose** – possessive
>   form of who

• Circle the correct word choice in the following sentences.

1. (Whose, Who's) party did you attend?

2. We had (all ready, already) made the turn when we realized our mistake.

3. A reunion is a great time to get everyone (all together, altogether).

4. Leave that package (their, there) where you found it.

5. My team is much better (than, then) yours.

6. (Its, It's) just the way he plays the game.

7. (Whose, Who's) that student at the end of the hall?

8. We were (all ready, already) to go when we saw the flat tire.

9. We were not (all together, altogether) pleased with that book.

10. (Their, There) luggage was lost somewhere in the terminal.

11. If I pay for the tickets, (then, than) will you go?

12. (Their, They're) going to the baseball game.

13. (Its, It's) still raining.

14. The dog did not like (its, it's) collar.

15. I (already, all ready) have a dog.

16. I like tomato soup better (then, than) chicken noodle soup.

17. (Who's Whose) jacket is this?

18. The football is over (there, their).

 IF8732 Grammar 7–8

More Problem Pairs

Certain pairs of words are often confused. The best defense against making a mistake with these words is to consult a dictionary.

brake– a mechanism for slowing down or stopping; **break** – to shatter or come apart
later – more late; **latter** – the second of two persons or things mentioned
lead – to go first, or a heavy metal; **led** – past tense of "lead"
loose – free, not tight; **lose** – to suffer the loss of
principal – head of a school, or important; **principle** – a rule of conduct, or a basic truth
plane – a flat surface, or an airplane; **plain** – not fancy, or a large area of flat land

• Circle the correct word choice in the following sentences.

1. The student driver missed the (break, brake) with his foot.

2. We will be going (later, latter) than you.

3. The room was lined with (led, lead) to protect the technician from the x-rays.

4. I went to the dentist because my tooth was (lose, loose).

5. The (principal, principle) works hard for her school.

6. She (led, lead) the way in the field of chemical engineering.

7. You don't have anything to (lose, loose).

8. I believe it is important to understand the (principle, principal) of gravity.

9. The glass will (break, brake) if you bump into it.

10. Henry thought that the (later, latter) of the two reasons made more sense.

11. The (plane, plain) was forced to make an emergency landing.

12. My tastes run to very (plain, plane) designs.

13. I will tell you about my problem (later, latter).

14. Follow these (principles, principals), and you will be a success.

15. The science students rolled the marble down the inclined (plain, plane).

16. We don't want the tigers to (loose, lose) their freedom.

17. The inspectors checked for traces of (lead, led) in the water.

18. The helicopter landed easily on the (plane, plain).

Answer Key
Grammar
Grades 7-8

Sentences and Fragments

> A sentence is a group of words which expresses a complete thought.
> We went to the party.
> Will you go to the party with me?
> A fragment is a group of words punctuated like a sentence but not expressing a complete thought.
> When we left the party.
> And then the cake.

- Write **S** before each group of words that is a sentence. Write **F** before each group of words that is a fragment.

_S_ 1. You should go to the doctor for a physical.
_S_ 2. A visit to the dentist makes me nervous.
_F_ 3. Shots in the arm.
_F_ 4. People in the waiting room.
_S_ 5. Always tell the doctor exactly where it hurts.
_F_ 6. When the nurse comes in.
_S_ 7. Did you have any cavities this time?
_S_ 8. The surgery was successful.
_F_ 9. If you go to the hospital.
_S_ 10. He filled out the medical form incorrectly.
_F_ 11. Then the doctor.
_S_ 12. Are you feeling better now?
_S_ 13. I feel wonderful!
_S_ 14. Please make me some more soup.

- Add words either before or after the following fragments to construct complete sentences.

1. When I broke my arm. _____ Sentences will vary. _____

2. If you go to visit Henry. _____

3. To mend his broken bone. _____

Recognizing Sentences

> A sentence expresses a complete thought. It should begin with a capital letter and end with a period (.), question mark (?), or exclamation point (!).

- Look at the examples below and underline the sentences. If a group of words is not a sentence, add words to make it a sentence and write the sentence on the line.

1. Portugal is in Europe.

2. On the same peninsula as Spain.
   Sentence will vary.

3. Both countries occupy the Iberian Peninsula.

4. Bordered by the Mediterranean Sea and the Atlantic Ocean, with water on three sides.
   Sentence will vary.

5. Portugal is much smaller than Spain.

6. It has a different language, although Portuguese is similar to Spanish.

7. Because both languages are based on Latin.
   Sentence will vary.

8. Why do you want to go to Portugal?

9. To see the beautiful scenery, which is world famous.
   Sentence will vary.

10. Visiting Portugal has always been my dream.

- In each example below, use the words to make a sentence. Remember that each sentence must express a complete thought, begin with a capital letter, and end with a period, question mark or exclamation point.

Sentences will vary.

1. boy, dog, fast

2. shellfish, cooked, rice _____

3. difficult, sentences, long, written _____

4. where, Spain, asked _____

Simple Subjects and Predicates

> The simple subject names the person or thing the sentence is about. It does not include articles or modifying words.
> The girl in the red hat ran to the corner.
> The simple predicate tells what the subject is or does. It does not include any modifying words. The simple predicate is a verb or a verb phrase.
> The main city library is expanding its shelves.
> John Maynard Keynes was an economist.

- In each of the following sentences, underline the simple subject once and the simple predicate twice.

1. One African bird is named the honey guide.
2. The favorite food of the honey guide is beeswax from the nests of wild bees.
3. The nests are too strong for the honey guide, though.
4. So the clever bird enlists the aid of an ally.
5. The unlikely ally is an animal called the ratel.
6. The black and white ratel is called the "honey badger" by many people.
7. Rich, sweet honey is the ratel's favorite food.
8. The ratel's thick, loose skin resists bee stings.
9. The smart bird finds a bees' nest.
10. It chatters to the ratel.
11. The chattering bird leads the ratel to the nest.
12. The ratel breaks the nest with its strong claws.
13. The hungry animal eats the honey.
14. Then the happy bird eats the wax from the broken nest.

© Carson-Dellosa   103   IF8732 Grammar 7–8

Complete Subjects and Predicates

Name _____

The **complete subject** of a sentence tells what the sentence is about. It may be one word or many words.
<u>The boy from Michigan</u> is the world geography champion.
<u>He</u> knew the answer to every question they asked him.
The **complete predicate** tells what the subject is or does. It may be one word or many words.
He <u>knew the answer to every question they asked him.</u>
The young student <u>won</u>.

- In the sentences below, underline the complete subjects once and the complete predicates twice.

1. The people in many parts of the world are unable to feed themselves in times of disaster.
2. International relief agencies and many governments try to send aid to those people.
3. The most famous international relief agency is the Red Cross.
4. The Red Cross was founded in 1864 to aid victims of war.
5. Red Cross workers fight misery in times of both war and peace.
6. Over 135 nations have Red Cross societies.
7. Each Red Cross society runs its own program.
8. The American Red Cross has more than 10 million volunteers.
9. Voluntary contributions fund the programs and services of the American Red Cross.
10. All aid to disaster victims is free.

- Write a short paragraph about an organization whose purpose you admire. In each sentence underline the complete subjects once and the complete predicates twice.

Paragraphs will vary.

Compound Subjects and Predicates

Name _____

A **compound subject** contains two or more subjects usually joined by *and* or *or*.
<u>Mark Twain</u> and <u>Harper Lee</u> are American authors.
A **compound predicate** has two or more predicates usually joined by *and, or,* or *but*.
They <u>wrote great novels</u> and <u>became famous</u>.

- In each of the following sentences, turn the subject into a compound subject and write the new sentence on the line. If necessary, change the verb to agree with the compound subject. For instance, "Anne <u>plays</u> softball," but "Anne and Toni <u>play</u> softball."

1. Mary is the best student in math class.   *Sentences will vary.*
2. Sycamore trees are my favorite trees.
3. Birds live in trees.
4. Light is necessary for a plant to grow.
5. Anna is my best friend.
6. Charlie is on the baseball team.

- In each of the following sentences, turn the predicate into a compound predicate using **and, or,** or **but**. Write the new sentence on the line.

1. Kristy dribbled to the foul line.   *Sentences will vary.*
2. Tom painted a picture for the show.
3. My father lit the barbecue.
4. Earl bought a new CD.

Declarative Sentences

Name _____

A **declarative sentence** makes a statement and ends with a period.
The sky is blue.
The car drove past slowly.
There are ducks in Central Park.

- For each of these declarative sentences, circle the words that should be capitalized and add punctuation.

1. (an) avalanche struck the village.
2. (the) snow swept down the mountain.
3. (many) homes were damaged.
4. (avalanche) warnings were given by the Forest Service.
5. (the) people of the village were evacuated in time.
6. (the) avalanche carried rock debris with it onto the highway.
7. (it) was believed to have been started by a car backfiring.
8. (fortunately) not one person was injured.
9. (there) is a lot of avalanche research being done in Switzerland.
10. (everyone) should be aware of the potential dangers of avalanches.
11. (an) avalanche is a mass of snow that slides down a mountain slope.
12. (most) avalanches result from weather conditions.

- Write five declarative sentences about a tornado, a hurricane, or a flood.

1. *Sentences will vary.*
2. _____
3. _____
4. _____
5. _____

Interrogative Sentences

Name _____

An **interrogative sentence** asks a question and ends with a question mark.
Where is the truck?
What time is the game?
When will we be going?

- For each of these interrogative sentences, circle the words that should be capitalized and add punctuation.

1. (were) you born in Canada ?
2. (what) form of government does Canada have ?
3. (what) is their monetary unit ?
4. (when) did you travel to Canada for your vacation ?
5. (what) languages do Canadians speak ?
6. (is) it a beautiful country ?

- Change the following declarative sentences into interrogative sentences by changing some of the words, the word order, the capitalization, and the punctuation. For example: "He told me the answer." becomes "Did he tell me the answer?"

1. I like ice cream.   *Sentences will vary.*
2. We are going to the beach.
3. Jake caught 30 fish from the pier.
4. Sun block is the most important thing to remember to bring.
5. There were no seagulls visible on the beach.
6. The waves crashed against the shore.
7. The sun glowed on the horizon.

© Carson-Dellosa   **104**   IF8732 Grammar 7–8

Imperative Sentences

An imperative sentence commands or requests. It ends with a period or an exclamation point. The subject "you" is understood.
  Don't try it!
  Please walk the dog.
  Fill the collection basket.

- For each of these imperative sentences, circle the word that should be capitalized and add punctuation.

1. (find) out how this problem should be solved.
2. (get) out of the way!
3. (please) drive defensively.
4. (clean) your room.
5. (please) try to understand my point of view.
6. (don't) walk on the grass.
7. (please) pack me a picnic lunch.
8. (don't) try this at home!
9. (start) the car and let it idle.
10. (cook) the fish and serve it to your friends.

Punctuation may vary.

- Write five imperative statements that a science teacher might make during a science lab. Be sure to use proper capitalization and punctuation. Do not use quotation marks.

1. _____ Sentences will vary. _____
2. _____
3. _____
4. _____
5. _____

Exclamatory Sentences

An exclamatory sentence can be either a statement or a command made with strong feeling. It ends with an exclamation point.
  Hold it right there!
  Stop!
  Don't believe it!

- For each of these exclamatory sentences, circle the word that must be capitalized and add punctuation.

1. (look) at that!
2. (this) is my favorite food!
3. (what) a terrific play we saw!
4. (it's) a home run!
5. (my) brother passed the exam!
6. (grandmother) is coming to visit!
7. (what) a fantastic day that was!
8. (we) won!
9. (what) an exquisite painting that is!
10. (this) is the most amazing thing that has ever happened to me!

- Write five exclamatory sentences you might hear at a baseball, basketball, or football game.

1. _____ Sentences will vary. _____
2. _____
3. _____
4. _____
5. _____

Recognizing Kinds of Sentences

There are four kinds of sentences: declarative, interrogative, imperative, and exclamatory.
Declarative sentences make a statement and end with a period.
  The sky is blue.
Interrogative sentences ask a question and end with a question mark.
  What color is the sky?
Imperative sentences command or request and end with a period or an exclamation point.
  Paint the sky blue on your mural.
Exclamatory sentences either make a statement or a command with strong feeling and end with an exclamation point.
  That's the bluest sky I've ever seen!

- Label the following sentences declarative (D), interrogative (IN), imperative (IM), or exclamatory (E).

D 1. Clouds are the best free show in the world.
IN 2. How can you say that?
IM/E 3. Just look at them!
D 4. They all look the same to me, I'm afraid.
IM 5. Pay attention while I show you the differences.
D 6. Those big, white clouds are cumulus clouds.
IN 7. Did you know that the ones that look like strands of hair are called cirrus clouds?
D 8. Stratus clouds look like they're in layers, or strata.
D 9. Nimbus clouds are rain clouds.
E 10. They are my favorites!
IN 11. What kinds of clouds are in the sky today?
IN 12. Is rain on the way?
D 13. The clouds are blocking the sun.
E 14. Jets fly right through them!

- Write one of each type of sentence about a trip on a plane.

1. (declarative) _____ Sentences will vary. _____
2. (interrogative) _____
3. (imperative) _____
4. (exclamatory) _____

Changing Sentences

- Below are 12 answers written as declarative sentences. Write the questions for those answers in the form of interrogative sentences.
  Example: "The sky is blue." The question might be this: "What color is the sky?"

1. My favorite sculptor is Michelangelo. *Questions will vary.*
2. His full name was Michelangelo Buonarroti.
3. He was from Italy.
4. He is also famous for his paintings and architecture.
5. His most famous piece of sculpture is the "Pietà."
6. He also sculpted a famous statue called "David."
7. He lived from 1475 to 1564.
8. He died in the middle of the 16th century.
9. His most famous paintings are on the ceiling of the Sistine Chapel.
10. They have recently been restored to their original colors.
11. It took several years to complete the restoration.
12. The Sistine Chapel is located in Vatican City.

- Write four types of sentences about another famous artist.

1. (declarative) _____ Sentences will vary. _____
2. (interrogative) _____
3. (imperative) _____
4. (exclamatory) _____

---

105   IF8732 Grammar 7–8

Simple and Compound Sentences

A **simple sentence** contains one independent clause.
  John walked into the center of town.
  The train whistled past.
  The doctor is in.
A **compound sentence** contains two independent clauses which are closely related. A conjunction usually joins the two clauses. Remember to put a comma after the first clause and before the conjunction that joins the two clauses.
  The team played hard, and they won the game easily.
  Soccer is a low scoring game, but it is very exciting.
  The forward kicked the ball, and the goalie grabbed it.

• Identify simple sentences (**S**) and compound sentences (**C**) by writing an **S** or **C** in each blank. Then, underline the simple subjects once and the simple predicates twice.

C 1. The Chartres Cathedral is a masterpiece of Gothic architecture, and it has become a famous landmark.

S 2. The town of Chartres is built on the bank of the Eure River.

C 3. Chartres is located in north-central France, and it is the capital of Eure-et-Loire.

S 4. The cathedral has two bell towers.

C 5. Cathedrals of this type were often the focal point of the community, and people sometimes devoted their entire lives to the construction of these religious buildings.

C 6. A fire in the year 1194 destroyed most of the cathedral, but it was rebuilt between 1194 and 1230.

• Write two simple sentences and two compound sentences about other famous buildings.

1. (simple) _____ *Sentences will vary.* _____

2. (simple) _____

3. (compound) _____

4. (compound) _____

Complex Sentences

A **complex sentence** contains one independent clause and one or more dependent clauses.
  (The independent clauses are underlined once; the dependent, twice.)
  The fish jumped over the dam when the wave crested.
  If you go to the store, buy me a candy bar.
  The carpenter who built this house is my brother.

• In the following complex sentences, underline the independent clauses once and the dependent clauses twice.

1. The astronauts left the vehicle when the solar panel failed.

2. The United States became serious about space exploration when the Soviet Union launched Sputnik 1.

3. If there is life on the moon, humans have not succeeded in finding it.

4. When a spacecraft is put in orbit, many people share the credit.

5. John Glenn, who was the first American to orbit the earth, became a senator.

6. The Apollo program had a lunar module that was capable of landing on the moon and returning to the main vehicle.

7. The Sputnik 1, which was launched in 1957, was the first artificial satellite.

8. When Neil Armstrong stepped onto the lunar surface, he was fulfilling a promise made by President Kennedy earlier in the decade.

9. The United States launched the space shuttle Columbia, which was the first reusable manned spacecraft.

10. The Challenger, which had seven astronauts on board, exploded in midair.

11. Because this disaster was so devastating, all missions were temporarily stopped.

• Write three complex sentences which tell about space exploration.

1. _____ *Sentences will vary.* _____

2. _____

3. _____

Compound/Complex Sentences

A **compound/complex sentence** contains two or more independent clauses and at least one dependent clause.
  The independent clauses are underlined once; the dependent, twice.
  When the game was over, Seth took the ball, and Larry threw it into the stands.

• In these compound/complex sentences, underline the independent clauses once and the dependent clauses twice.

1. If you have a solution, let us know, and we will try it.

2. Because Trudy had studied previous chess matches, she was able to play brilliantly, and she beat Sid soundly.

3. When we get to the park, Bill will put up the tent, and Carl will start the fire.

4. Though the steak was not fully cooked, Judy cut it, and Ned ate it.

5. Wendell had never gone to college, and he worked at the factory until he won a scholarship.

6. The food was free, and the people who came enjoyed it.

7. Though it was brand new, the stereo would not play, and it destroyed my tape.

8. Because Jenny broke her arm, she could not play in the concert, and the orchestra sounded terrible.

9. Sara suggested the movie, and Elliot and Michael agreed when they heard her choice.

10. Steven went back to Florida, where he opened a law firm, but it was not a financial success.

11. The enraged inventor sued the company, but when he finally won his case, he was deeply in debt.

• In a book or magazine find three examples of compound/complex sentences. Write them here.

1. _____ *Sentences will vary.* _____

2. _____

3. _____

Recognizing Sentence Types

A **simple sentence** contains one independent clause.
A **compound sentence** contains two independent clauses joined by a conjunction. Remember to put a comma after the first clause and before the conjunction that joins them.
A **complex sentence** contains one independent clause and one or more dependent clauses.
A **compound/complex sentence** contains two or more independent clauses and at least one dependent clause.

• Identify the following sentences as Simple (**S**), Compound (**C**), Complex (**CX**), or Compound/Complex (**C/CX**).

C/CX 1. Whenever a new video game is developed, we immediately go to the store, and my mom looks it over carefully.

C 2. The car hit the tree, but there was no damage.

C/CX 3. If the camping trip is cancelled, Jake will stay home, but Colleen will probably go to a movie.

CX 4. When you get to the store, you will be given a free gift.

C/CX 5. The teacher, who tried to take charge, was very stern, but the class didn't pay much attention to him.

S 6. Kevin tried to get the pump started.

C 7. The disc jockey was on the air, and his replacement was waiting in the next room.

C 8. A city must be planned carefully, or people will not want to live in it.

C 9. We were going to attend the game, but it started raining.

C 10. I am going to do my homework after school, but I would rather play with my friends.

C 11. Sheila put a dollar into the pop machine, but nothing came out.

S 12. The book was exciting and easy to read.

C 13. Harry sang the song for his mom, and she loved it.

C/CX 14. Because the computer was a very expensive purchase, Dad bought a special table for it, and he kept it in an air-conditioned room.

Fragments

A sentence contains a subject and a verb and expresses a complete thought. A group of words that is punctuated like a sentence but does not contain a complete thought is called a fragment. Often the reason the fragment does not express a complete thought is that it lacks a subject or verb.
Fragments:
Went home past the supermarket.
The reason I missed school yesterday.
Because I wanted.
And her brother.
Sometimes you can correct a fragment by adding a word or words. Other times you can make the correction by connecting the fragment to a sentence and changing the punctuation.
Incorrect: On the way to school, I saw Amy. And her brother.
Correct: On the way to school, I saw Amy and her brother.

- Correct each of the fragments below by adding a word or words to make a complete sentence. Change capital letters and punctuation where necessary.

Sentences will vary.

1. Jim, who is the best player on the team.

2. Opened the package and put it carefully on the table.

3. Jumped straight up and scored the basket.

4. Changing the way we do things.

5. Promised me I could have it for a week.

- Correct each of the fragments below by connecting it to the accompanying sentence. Change capital letters and punctuation where necessary. *Sentences will vary.*

1. Many people don't like abstract art. Because they don't understand it.

2. The abstract movement was started by a number of gifted artists. Like Miró and Kandinsky.

3. They thought art was becoming too realistic. Looking just like photography.

4. Some photographers also joined. Looking for new ways to see the world.

Page 16

Run-ons

A run-on is two or more complete sentences written without proper punctuation between them.
Run-ons: Ballet is exhausting work, you have to be in great shape to be a dancer.
It looks easy it's really hard.
It's beautiful, though, ballet is my favorite activity.
Run-ons can be corrected in three ways.
1. If the two sentences are closely related, they can be separated by a semi-colon.
Correct: Ballet is exhausting work; you have to be in great shape to be a dancer.
2. Closely related sentences can also be separated with a comma and a conjunction.
Correct: It looks easy, but it's really hard.
3. Sentences that are not as closely related can be separated with a period.
It's beautiful, though. Ballet is my favorite activity.

- Correct the run-ons below by rewriting the sentences correctly. If a sentence is not a run-on, write OK next to it. *Sentences may vary.*

1. Studying leaves is fascinating there are so many different kinds.
Studying leaves is fascinating. There are so many....

2. Leaves come in different shades of green no two kinds seem to be the same.
Leaves come in different shades of green, and no two kinds....

3. Leaves that grow in low light are usually dark green leaves that grow in bright light are lighter green.
Leaves that grow in low light are usually dark green. Leaves....

4. A leaf's shape is important experts can tell a lot about a tree from the shape of its leaves.
A leaf's shape is important. Experts can tell a lot....

5. Leaves from rain forest plants often have drip tips these are pointed tips that help water run off the leaf.
Leaves from rainforest plants often have drip tips; these are....

6. Some leaves have complicated shapes these shapes allow the wind to blow the leaf without tearing it.
Some leaves have complicated shapes; these shapes allow....

7. Desert plants' leaves often have a waxy coating this helps them to conserve water.
Desert plants' leaves often have a waxy coating; this helps....

_OK_ 8. Hormones and the amount of daylight a plant receives can affect plant growth.

Page 17

Inverted Sentence Order

Sometimes part or all of the verb comes before the subject in a sentence. Sentences in which this happens are called inverted sentences. Inverted means that the order is reversed.
Is Bill finished with the dictionary?
On the corner is the best ice-cream store in town.
Have you heard the new CD yet?
If you had trouble finding the subject and predicate in any of those sentences, try rearranging the subject and predicate.
Bill is finished with the dictionary.
The best ice-cream store in town is on the corner.
You have heard the new CD yet.

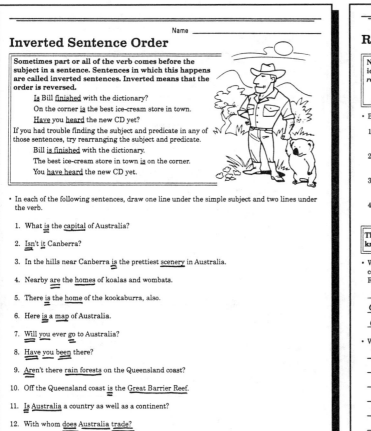

- In each of the following sentences, draw one line under the simple subject and two lines under the verb.

1. What is the capital of Australia?

2. Isn't it Canberra?

3. In the hills near Canberra is the prettiest scenery in Australia.

4. Nearby are the homes of koalas and wombats.

5. There is the home of the kookaburra, also.

6. Here is a map of Australia.

7. Will you ever go to Australia?

8. Have you been there?

9. Aren't there rain forests on the Queensland coast?

10. Off the Queensland coast is the Great Barrier Reef.

11. Is Australia a country as well as a continent?

12. With whom does Australia trade?

Page 18

Recognizing Nouns

Nouns are words that name people, places, things, or ideas. Nouns are words that identify—that person is **John**, that place is **home**, that thing is a **ball**, or that idea is **responsibility**.
kite, president, bell, book, candle, freedom, ships, shoes, democracy, Crazy Horse, doctor, house, park

- Below each of the nouns, write whether the noun names a person, place, thing, or idea.

1. rock — thing
2. firefighter — person
3. China — place
4. book — thing
5. Lucy Van Pelt — person
6. jet — thing
7. Michigan — place
8. pen — thing
9. tree — thing
10. rage — idea
11. Rachel Carson — person
12. boat — thing
13. happiness — idea
14. Tennessee — place
15. joy — idea
16. emotion — idea

The words **a**, **an**, and **the** are often used before nouns. These words are known as articles.

- Write the correct article (**a** or **an**) to go with each of the nouns below. If the noun begins with a consonant sound, use the article **a**. If the noun begins with a vowel sound, use the article **an**. Remember, it is the sound not the spelling which helps you make this determination.

a book
an hour
a classroom
an eagle
a tiger
a penguin
a sea
a keyboard
an exclamation
a President
an idea
an opera

- Write a short paragraph about an issue that is in the news. Underline each noun that you use.

Paragraph will vary.

Page 19

Page 20

Recognizing Nouns: Suffixes

> A word ending is called a suffix. The following suffixes are sometimes used to end nouns: -hood, -dom, -ment, -ance, -ness, -er, -or.
> childhood, earldom, excitement, appearance, illness, teacher, animator

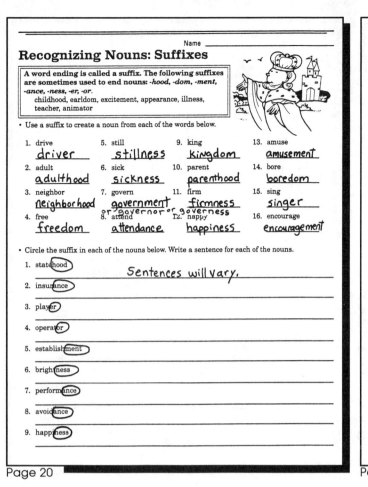

• Use a suffix to create a noun from each of the words below.

1. drive — **driver**
2. adult — **adulthood**
3. neighbor — **neighborhood**
4. free — **freedom**
5. still — **stillness**
6. sick — **sickness**
7. govern — **government** or **governor** or **governess**
8. attend — **attendance**
9. king — **kingdom**
10. parent — **parenthood**
11. firm — **firmness**
12. happy — **happiness**
13. amuse — **amusement**
14. bore — **boredom**
15. sing — **singer**
16. encourage — **encouragement**

• Circle the suffix in each of the nouns below. Write a sentence for each of the nouns.

1. state(hood) — Sentences will vary.
2. insur(ance)
3. play(er)
4. oper(ator)
5. establish(ment)
6. bright(ness)
7. perform(ance)
8. avoid(ance)
9. happi(ness)

Page 20

Page 21

Common and Proper Nouns

> Proper nouns are the names of particular persons, places, or things. They are spelled with capital letters. Your name is a proper noun.
> New York City, Babe Ruth, Clara Barton, Empire State Building
>
> All other nouns are called common nouns. Common nouns do not name particular persons, places, or things.
> city, athlete, nurse, building

• If the word listed below is a proper noun, write the common noun that describes it. If it is a common noun, give an example of a proper noun that matches the word. Underline the proper noun in each pair of words.
Examples: <u>Babe Ruth</u>: athlete
city: <u>Los Angeles</u>

Answers will vary

1. car: _____
2. teacher: _____
3. <u>Abraham Lincoln</u>: **president**
4. <u>Mayflower</u>: **ship**
5. country: _____
6. <u>Michael</u>: **boy/man**
7. girl: _____
8. <u>Big Mac</u>: **sandwich**
9. <u>Dan Rather</u>: **anchorman**
10. actress: _____
11. <u>Mark Twain</u>: **author**
12. constellation: _____
13. <u>Buddhism</u>: **religion**
14. <u>Mt. Everest</u>: **mountain**
15. <u>St. Louis</u>: **city**
16. <u>*New York Times*</u>: **newspaper**

• Choose five sets of nouns above. For each pair of words, write one sentence that uses both the proper and the common noun correctly.

1. Sentences will vary.
2. _____
3. _____
4. _____
5. _____

Page 21

Page 22

Abstract and Concrete Nouns

> A concrete noun names something that can be seen or touched.
> bridge, shell, car
> An abstract noun names an idea, quality, or state of mind.
> liberty, intelligence, happiness

• Label the following words as concrete (C) or abstract (A).

C 1. fence
A 2. success
C 3. Dr. Smith
A 4. sadness
A 5. research
C 6. desk
C 7. Columbia River
C 8. hat
C 9. walnuts
A 10. imagination
A 11. forgetfulness
C 12. telephone

• In the following sentences circle the concrete nouns and underline the abstract nouns.

1. (Mount Everest) located in (Tibet) is the highest (mountain) on (earth)
2. Tibetan (nomads) must exert a lot of <u>energy</u> in their daily <u>struggle</u> to live.
3. One <u>skill</u> they possess is <u>horsemanship</u>.
4. Becoming a Buddhist (monk) is considered a high <u>honor</u> among the Tibetan (people).
5. The (Dalai Lama) Tibet's <u>leader</u>, is considered an <u>inspiration</u> to his (people)
6. (Tibet) has far fewer (monasteries) today than it did in the past.
7. The (monks) in the (monasteries) encourage <u>education</u>, <u>art</u>, and <u>worship</u>.

• List three abstract nouns and three concrete nouns. Nouns will vary.

1. (abstract) _____   1. (concrete) _____
2. (abstract) _____   2. (concrete) _____
3. (abstract) _____   3. (concrete) _____

Page 22

Page 23

Plural Nouns

> Plural means more than one. To form the plural of most nouns, just add -s.
> book, books; time, times; house, houses; lesson, lessons
> If a noun ends in s, x, ch, z, sh, or ss, add -es.
> bus, buses; fox, foxes; lunch, lunches; waltz, waltzes; dish, dishes; boss, bosses

• Write sentences using the plural forms of the nouns listed. Sentences will vary.

1. pilot, airplane (include pilots and airplanes)
2. box, square (include boxes and squares)
3. team, bus (include teams and buses)
4. boss, job (include bosses and jobs)
5. window, tree (include windows and trees)
6. book, class (include books and classes)
7. batter, hit (include batters and hits)
8. cloud, wish (include clouds and wishes)
9. lesson, suffix (include lessons and suffixes)
10. branch, root (include branches and roots)

• Write three sentences each of which includes at least one singular noun and one plural noun. Underline the singular nouns and circle the plural nouns.

1. Sentences will vary.
2. _____
3. _____

Page 23

More Plural Nouns

To form the plural of nouns that end in a *y* preceded by a consonant, change the *y* to *i* and add -*es*.
baby, babies

For nouns that end in a *y* preceded by a vowel, just add -*s*.
key, keys

To form the plural of a word that ends in an *o* preceded by a vowel, add -*s*. For words that end in an *o* preceded by a consonant, usually add -*es*. (Check a dictionary if you're unsure.)
folio, folios; tomato, tomatoes

For words that end in *f* or *fe*, sometimes change the *f* to *v* and add -*es*; other times just add -*s* (Consult a dictionary if you're unsure.)
knife, knives; safe, safes; chief, chiefs

• Write the plural form next to each singular noun in the list below.

1. monkey — monkeys
2. class — classes
3. tax — taxes
4. berry — berries
5. loaf — loaves
6. latch — latches
7. fez — fezzes
8. wish — wishes
9. hoof — hooves or hoofs
10. galley — galleys
11. shoe — shoes
12. wax — waxes
13. horse — horses
14. roof — roofs
15. puff — puffs
16. honey — honeys
17. color — colors
18. waltz — waltzes
19. wife — wives
20. victory — victories
21. potato — potatoes
22. tress — tresses
23. story — stories
24. avocado — avocados

Note: There are some words that don't follow any rules—their plurals just have to be learned. For instance, *deer* and *species* are spelled the same whether singular or plural. Feeling confused? When in doubt, always check your dictionary.

Check your dictionary and write the plural form for each of these nouns.

1. crisis — crises
2. brother-in-law — brothers-in-law
3. man — men
4. ox — oxen
5. spoonful — spoonfuls
6. datum — data

Gender of Nouns

Gender refers to the sex indicated by the noun. The four genders are masculine, which indicates the male sex; feminine, which indicates the female sex; neuter, which indicates no sex; and indefinite, which means the gender could be either male or female.
masculine—actor, king,
feminine—actress, queen
neuter—car, boat
indefinite—assistant, teacher

• Label each noun below according to the correct gender. Write **M** for masculine, **F** for feminine, **N** for neuter, and **I** for indefinite.

N 1. carpet
M 2. knight
F 3. niece
F 4. filly
I 5. lamb
N 6. doorknob
F 7. waitress
F 8. grandmother
I 9. President
N 10. automobile
M 11. uncle
M 12. brother
N 13. dam
I 14. doctor
F 15. empress
I 16. giraffe
F 17. princess
F 18. goddess
I 19. gopher
I 20. jellyfish
F 21. heiress
I 22. gourmet
M 23. emperor
M 24. grandson
N 25. river
N or I 26. pitcher
I 27. goat

• Write a short paragraph explaining how a woman's position in society has changed in recent years. In your paragraph, place an **M** above the nouns that are masculine, an **F** above those that are feminine, an **N** above those that are neuter, and an **I** above those that are indefinite.

Paragraph will vary.

Possessive Nouns

Nouns that show ownership are called possessive nouns.
To form the possessive of a singular noun, add an apostrophe and an *s* (-'s).
Tom's bell, the author's book, society's values

To form the possessive of a plural noun, add only an apostrophe if the word ends in *s*.
the authors' books, the Nortons' home

If the plural of the noun does not end in *s*, add an apostrophe and an *s* ('s).
men's race, children's hour

• Write the possessive of the following nouns.

1. woman — woman's
2. mice — mice's
3. horses — horses'
4. girls — girls'
5. teacher — teacher's
6. umbrella — umbrella's
7. princess — princess's
8. home — home's
9. players — players'
10. students — students'
11. host — host's
12. country — country's
13. presidents — presidents'
14. scissors — scissors'
15. Schindler — Schindler's
16. leaves — leaves'
17. witnesses — witnesses'
18. actress — actress's
19. statue — statue's
20. pants — pants'
21. river — river's
22. company — company's
23. nurse — nurse's
24. states — states'

• Write a short paragraph describing some of your and your family's favorite possessions. Underline the possessive nouns.

Paragraph will vary.

Collective Nouns

A collective noun names a group of persons, places, or things.
band, team, audience, United States
When a collective noun refers to the group as a unit, the noun is considered singular.
The family went on vacation.
The flock headed on its northern course.
When a collective noun refers to the individual members of the group who are acting separately, the noun is considered plural.
The class brought their pets to show and tell.
The family are all going their separate ways.

• Indicate whether the collective nouns in the following sentences are singular (**S**) or plural (**P**). Circle the correct word if there is a choice to be made.

S 1. The jury filed out of the courtroom.
S 2. The family (is, are) going on vacation to Georgia.
S 3. All during the game the crowd (was, were) very enthusiastic.
S 4. The team (is, are) getting on the bus after (its, their) heartbreaking loss.
P 5. The school staff worked throughout the summer on (its, their) lesson plans.
S 6. That group of spectators (is, are) getting awfully rowdy.
S 7. The symphony (is, are) playing some of the old favorites.
S 8. The set of books fell from the shelf.
P 9. The audience (is, are) returning to (its, their) cars.
P 10. The staff (was, were) happy about (its, their) bonuses.

• Write a short paragraph using at least three collective nouns. Write **P** or **S** above each collective noun to show if it is singular or plural.

Paragraph will vary.

IF8732 Grammar 7–8

Predicate Nouns

> A predicate noun is a noun used as a subject complement. Predicate nouns follow linking verbs.
> Theodore Roosevelt was the <u>President</u> back then.

• In each of the following sentences, circle the linking verb and underline the predicate noun.

1. After his retirement, Mark became a <u>consultant</u>.
2. Uncle Earl was the best <u>storyteller</u> in the family.
3. Ben is a talented <u>student</u>.
4. Rick was <u>president</u> of the club last year.
5. St. Paul is the <u>capital</u> of Minnesota.
6. "The Raven" is the most popular <u>poem</u> in the anthology.
7. Mildred became an <u>authority</u> on fungi.
8. The President is the <u>commander in chief</u>.
9. Alaska became <u>part</u> of the United States in this century.
10. Melissa was a talented <u>sculptor</u>.
11. Grandfather became a <u>carpenter</u>.
12. The principal is <u>chairperson</u> of the committee.
13. The general was the <u>leader</u> of the army.
14. The boy was a <u>soldier</u> in the Civil War.

• Write four sentences using predicate nouns. Underline the predicate nouns.

1. _Sentences will vary._
2. _____
3. _____
4. _____

Direct Objects

> A direct object is a noun or pronoun that follows an action verb. It tells what or who receives the action of the verb.
> The flood washed out the <u>road</u>.
> To find the direct object, ask *who* or *what* after the action verb.
> Question: The flood washed out *what*?
> Answer: the *road* (direct object)

• In each of the following sentences, circle the action verb and underline the direct object.

1. The Polar Bears won the <u>championship</u>.
2. Darcy answered the <u>question</u>.
3. Without delay Jasper boarded the <u>train</u>.
4. The salesclerk in the department store sold every pink <u>shirt</u> in stock.
5. President Lincoln sent <u>General Grant</u> into the battle.
6. The student read the <u>newspaper</u> every day.
7. The three networks immediately sent <u>reporters</u> to the crime scene.
8. Marcel gave a <u>check</u> to the charitable organization.
9. The principal grabbed the <u>basketball</u>.
10. Father wants <u>us</u> to return the car as soon as possible.
11. The French teacher sponsors the <u>Honor Society</u>.
12. The enthusiastic boy joined the <u>team</u>.
13. Julie won the <u>prize</u> at the fair last summer.
14. The clown wearing the polka-dotted hat threw the <u>balloon</u>.
15. He chose <u>us</u> to go on the trip with Harry.

• Write three sentences, including a noun used as a direct object in each. Underline the direct object and circle the action verb.

Sentences will vary.
_____
_____

Indirect Objects

> An indirect object is a noun or pronoun that names the person *to whom* or *for whom* something is done.
> Martina served the <u>guests</u> raw fish.
> To find the indirect object, ask *to whom* or *for whom* after the action verb.
> Question: Martina served raw fish *to whom*?
> Answer: the *guests* (indirect object)

• In each of the following sentences, underline the indirect object and circle the action verb.

1. Paul told <u>him</u> the bad news.
2. The director taught the <u>choir</u> a new song.
3. Gerald gave <u>Sharon</u> a symbol of his love.
4. I sent <u>Barbara</u> a postcard from France.
5. The farmer fed the <u>geese</u> the corn.
6. The star goalie left <u>her</u> two tickets at the gate.
7. The boss handed his <u>employee</u> the broom.
8. The book won <u>her</u> instant fame.
9. The window in the office offered the <u>clients</u> a good view.
10. Mary offered the <u>secretary</u> a piece of cake.
11. Shelly gave <u>them</u> her trophy to put in the display case.

• Write three sentences, including an indirect object in each. Underline the indirect objects once, the direct objects twice, and circle the action verbs.

1. _Sentences will vary._
2. _____
3. _____

Objects of Prepositions

> A noun or pronoun used as the object of a preposition follows the preposition, though there may be modifiers of the noun coming between it and the preposition.
> She waited <u>in the *building*</u>.
> Marie gave the book <u>to *him*</u>.
> To find the object, ask *whom* or *what* after the preposition.
> She waited in *what*? the *building*
> Marie gave the book to *whom*? to *him*

• In each sentence, underline the entire prepositional phrase and circle the object of the preposition.

1. We all hoped <u>for something</u> exciting <u>under the Christmas tree</u>.
2. Santa's sleigh flew <u>over the house</u>.
3. Sara scurried <u>into a hiding place</u> she always reserved <u>for herself</u>.
4. I told her it was just St. Nick <u>on the roof</u>.
5. Her response was to crawl farther <u>under her bed</u>.
6. Now we could hear him <u>in the kitchen</u>.
7. Then I wondered why he was <u>in that part of the house</u>.
8. Just to be safe, I looked <u>in the phone book</u> and dialed the police.
9. Santa found a turkey sandwich <u>in the refrigerator</u>.
10. We had forgotten to put out cookies <u>for him</u>.
11. He was gone when the police pulled <u>onto the driveway</u>.

• Write three sentences about a holiday. Each sentence should include a prepositional phrase. Underline the entire prepositional phrase and circle the object of the preposition.

1. _Sentences will vary._
2. _____
3. _____

Appositives

An appositive is a noun or noun phrase placed next to or very near another noun or noun phrase to identify, explain, or supplement its meaning.
Mr. Lange, our English teacher, is very intelligent.

- In each of the following sentences, underline the appositive and circle the noun it explains.

1. Kerri, my older sister, left immediately.
2. His car, a vintage roadster, crashed.
3. That man, the village chief, will command.
4. Baseball, my favorite sport, ended yesterday.
5. The senator, a Democrat, voted today.
6. Mr. Tobias, our Latin teacher, was nominated and defeated.
7. His house, a rambling shack, burned down.
8. The dog, a huge German shepherd, jumped up.
9. The boat, a sleek cruiser, slid past.
10. My cat, a grey manx, stretched and yawned.
11. Did you see the film at Studio 28, the movie theater?
12. My favorite ice cream, butter pecan, was on sale.

- Write three sentences which include appositives about three famous people currently in the news.

1. _Sentences will vary._
2. _____
3. _____

Page 32

Recognition of Verbs

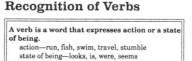 

A verb is a word that expresses action or a state of being.
action—run, fish, swim, travel, stumble
state of being—looks, is, were, seems

- In each of the following sentences, circle the verb and indicate if it is an action verb (A) or a state of being verb (B).

A 1. Powerful telescopes probe the remote reaches of the universe.
A 2. New technology strips away old limitations.
A 3. Computers adjust the optics.
B 4. Hawaii's Keck Telescope is amazing.
B 5. The Milky Way is an example of a spiral galaxy.
A 6. The Milky Way contains hundreds of billions of stars.
B 7. A supernova is an exploding star.
B 8. A lot of knowledge about the galaxy is pure conjecture.

- Identify these verbs as action verbs (A) or state of being verbs (B).

A 1. hugs the child
B 2. was a pilot
A 3. threw the ball
A 4. baked a cake
B 5. am sorry
A 6. lifted the bar
B 7. seems cold
A 8. mail the letter
A 9. read a book
A 10. sings the song
B 11. looks pretty
B 12. is happy

- Write three sentences that contain action verbs and three that contain state of being verbs. Underline the action verbs once and the state of being verbs twice.

1. (action) _Sentences will vary._
2. (action) _____
3. (action) _____
4. (being) _____
5. (being) _____
6. (being) _____

Page 33

More Verbs

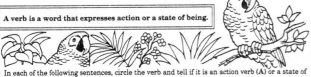

A verb is a word that expresses action or a state of being.

- In each of the following sentences, circle the verb and tell if it is an action verb (A) or a state of being verb (B).

B 1. Macaws are the largest of all parrots.
B 2. Their very long tails are unique in the parrot family.
B 3. Their wings are long and pointed.
A 4. Macaws eat fruit, nuts, and seeds.
A 5. The macaw screams loudly.
B 6. The macaw's coloring is spectacular.
B 7. The Scarlet macaw is the best known species.
A 8. Eighteen species of these parrots live in South America.
A 9. These birds are often poached.
A 10. People easily tame macaws.
B 11. Macaws' big beaks are extremely powerful.
A 12. These birds fly swiftly over the rain forest.
A 13. These large parrots nest in the holes of trees.
B 14. They are not common household pets.
A 15. Macaws live in forested areas.

- Write a short paragraph about a pet you would like to have. Include action and state of being verbs and circle them.

Paragraph will vary.
_____
_____
_____

Page 34

Active Voice Verbs

A verb is in the active voice when the subject is performing the action. (The subject is underlined once; the verb, twice.)
Ron changed his clothes.
The elephant fell from the stand.
The stone shattered his glasses.

- Each of these sentences contains an active verb. Underline the simple subject once and the verb twice.

1. Amelia Earhart flew alone over the Atlantic Ocean.
2. She made her crossing in 1932.
3. Amelia opened the field of aviation for many other women.
4. Ms. Earhart worked as a nurse's aide during World War I.
5. She earned a pilot's license by 1922.
6. She married George Putnam, a publisher.
7. This brave pilot tried to fly around the world in 1937.
8. Her plane disappeared during a flight over the Pacific Ocean.
9. Her mysterious disappearance fueled much speculation over the years.
10. Some people believe she drowned.
11. Her navigator also vanished.

- Write five sentences using active verbs about a trip you have taken. Underline the simple subjects once and the verbs twice.

1. _Sentences will vary._
2. _____
3. _____
4. _____
5. _____

Page 35

Passive Voice Verbs

A verb is in the passive voice when the subject is receiving the action. (The subject is underlined once; the verb, twice.)
The windows were cleaned by Roger.
The house was painted by professionals.
A lot of homework was given by the teacher.

- Change the following sentences using active verbs instead of passive verbs.

1. The people of France had been ruled by the aristocracy for centuries.
   The aristocracy ruled the people of France for centuries.

2. Louis XVI was blamed by the common people for new, burdensome taxes.
   The common people blamed Louis XVI for new, burdensome taxes.

3. In 1789 a royal fortress called the Bastille was stormed by a mob of angry Parisians.
   In 1789, a mob of angry Parisians stormed a royal fortress....

4. Royal troops were forced by the mob to withdraw from Paris.
   The mob forced royal troops to withdraw from Paris.

5. Later, the revolutionary French government was overthrown by Napoleon Bonaparte.
   Later, Napolean Bonaparte overthrew the revolutionary....

6. The central government was made strong through Napoleon's efficient administration.
   Napoleon's efficient administration made the central government strong.

7. Europe was nearly destroyed by Napoleon's ambition.
   Napoleon's ambition nearly destroyed Europe.

8. Napoleon was finally defeated by his enemies at the Battle of Waterloo.
   His enemies defeated Napoleon at the Battle of Waterloo.

9. The rest of Europe also was influenced by the French Revolution.
   The French Revolution influenced the rest of Europe.

- Write three sentences using passive verbs about an event in history.

1. _____ *Sentences will vary.*
2. _____
3. _____

Using Active and Passive Voice Verbs

A verb is in the active voice when the subject performs the action. A verb is in the passive voice when the subject receives the action.

Passive voice should be used sparingly. Active voice expresses action in a natural, more direct way.

- Identify the verbs in the following sentences as active (A) or passive (P). If the verb is passive voice, rewrite the sentence changing the verb to active voice.

P 1. The first pyramid in ancient Egypt was built around 2650 B.C. by the Egyptians.
Egyptians built the first pyramid in ancient Egypt around 2650 B.C.

A 2. The pharaohs constructed many temples in honor of the Egyptian gods.

P 3. The Egyptians were conquered by the Hyksos.
The Hyksos conquered the Egyptians.

A 4. The Hyksos used horses and chariots to defeat the Egyptian army.

A 5. The Egyptians learned to use the same tactics and drove the Hyksos out.

P 6. The course of Egyptian history was changed by Amenhotep IV.
Amenhotep IV changed the course of Egyptian history.

A 7. He worshiped a sun god called the Aton.

P 8. The Aton was represented as the disk of the sun.
The disk of the sun represented the Aton.

P 9. The capital of Egypt was moved to Akhetaton by the king.
The king moved the capital of Egypt to Akhetaton.

A 10. Several other changes by the king angered many Egyptians.

- Write four sentences about ancient Egypt using the type of verb that is indicated.

1. (active) _____ *Sentences will vary.*
2. (passive) _____
3. (active) _____
4. (passive) _____

Verb Phrases

A verb phrase is a group of words that do the work of a single verb. The phrase includes one principal verb and one or more helping verbs.
The teacher was trying to control the class.

- In each of the following sentences, underline the verb phrase and circle the helping verbs.

1. Charles Darwin (was) born in 1809.
2. He (was) raised in Shrewsbury, England.
3. The theory of evolution (was) introduced by Charles Darwin in the 1850s.
4. Many people (are) attracted by the logic of the theory.
5. The theory (has been) refined over the years.
6. Darwin (was) exploring on the H.M.S. *Beagle* in 1831.
7. He (had) studied plant and animal life on his travels.
8. He (was) forming an explanation for the phenomena he observed.
9. His theory (was) supported by Alfred Russell Wallace, a noted British scientist.
10. Darwin (was) convinced that modern species evolved from earlier ones.
11. He (was) fascinated by the process of natural selection.
12. His place in history (was) strengthened by his book *The Origin of Species*.
13. Darwin's work (has had) influence on religious thought.
14. Many people (have) opposed his theories.
15. Other writers and scientists (have) referred to Darwin's ideas in their own work.

- Write four sentences about geography which contain verb phrases. Underline the verb phrases and circle the helping verbs.

1. _____ *Sentences will vary.*
2. _____
3. _____
4. _____

Regular Verbs

A regular verb is one which forms its past tense and past participle by adding -d or -ed to the present tense form.
walk, walked, (have/has/had) walked
try, tried, (have/has/had) tried
call, called, (have/has/had) called

- Write the past and the past participle forms of the following verbs.

Present	Past		Past Participle
1. crawl	crawled	(have, has, had)	crawled
2. skate	skated	(have, has, had)	skated
3. fish	fished	(have, has, had)	fished
4. climb	climbed	(have, has, had)	climbed
5. love	loved	(have, has, had)	loved
6. answer	answered	(have, has, had)	answered
7. travel	traveled	(have, has, had)	traveled
8. contend	contended	(have, has, had)	contended
9. pretend	pretended	(have, has, had)	pretended
10. develop	developed	(have, has, had)	developed

- Use each of the following verbs in a sentence of your own.

1. derive _____ *Sentences will vary.*
2. has commanded _____
3. have served _____
4. open _____
5. has watched _____
6. rule _____
7. have crashed _____
8. jump _____
9. has realized _____

IF8732 Grammar 7–8

Irregular Verbs

An irregular verb is any verb which does not form its past and past participle by adding -d or -ed to its present tense.
> begin, began, (has, have, had) begun
> lead, led, (has, have, had) led
> grow, grew, (has, have, had) grown

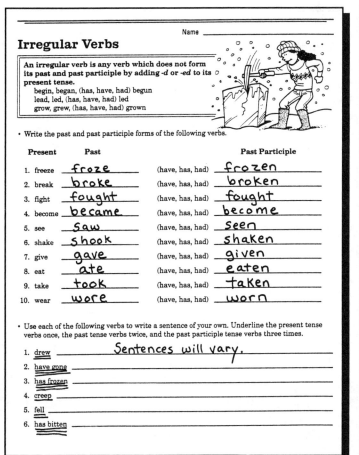

• Write the past and past participle forms of the following verbs.

Present	Past		Past Participle
1. freeze	froze	(have, has, had)	frozen
2. break	broke	(have, has, had)	broken
3. fight	fought	(have, has, had)	fought
4. become	became	(have, has, had)	become
5. see	saw	(have, has, had)	seen
6. shake	shook	(have, has, had)	shaken
7. give	gave	(have, has, had)	given
8. eat	ate	(have, has, had)	eaten
9. take	took	(have, has, had)	taken
10. wear	wore	(have, has, had)	worn

• Use each of the following verbs to write a sentence of your own. Underline the present tense verbs once, the past tense verbs twice, and the past participle tense verbs three times.

1. drew   Sentences will vary.
2. have gone
3. has frozen
4. creep
5. fell
6. has bitten

Page 40

Linking Verbs

A linking verb does not show action. It connects a word or words in the predicate to the subject in the sentence. Some very common linking verbs are forms of *be*: am, are, is, was, were.
> Father is a banker.
> I am a student.

• In each of the following sentences, underline the linking verb and circle the two words that are joined by it.

1. Water is part of all living things.
2. Water molecules are simple in structure.
3. Water management is a complex problem.
4. A desert is a hot, barren region.
5. Desert living is common.
6. Farming is restricted.
7. Rainfall is scarce.
8. Water for cities is sometimes difficult to find.
9. States which lack water supplies are often desperate for help.
10. Nearby rivers are sources of water.
11. It is important to consider the ecological effects of any diversion of water.
12. Some desert areas are cold.
13. Most deserts are very hot.
14. The largest desert is the Sahara.

• Write four sentences about the geography of your state using a linking verb in each.

1. Sentences will vary.
2.
3.
4.

Page 41

More Linking Verbs

A linking verb does not show action. It connects a word or words in the predicate to the subject in the sentence. Forms of *be* are common linking verbs. Other linking verbs include *grow, look, became, appear, look, taste,* and *remain*.

Note: A verb is a linking verb if you can substitute the verb "is" or "was" for it.
> "The food tasted spicy."   "The food was spicy."

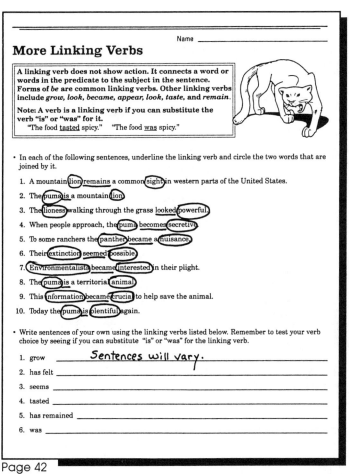

• In each of the following sentences, underline the linking verb and circle the two words that are joined by it.

1. A mountain lion remains a common sight in western parts of the United States.
2. The puma is a mountain lion.
3. The lioness walking through the grass looked powerful.
4. When people approach, the puma becomes secretive.
5. To some ranchers the panther became a nuisance.
6. Their extinction seemed possible.
7. Environmentalists became interested in their plight.
8. The puma is a territorial animal.
9. This information became crucial to help save the animal.
10. Today the puma is plentiful again.

• Write sentences of your own using the linking verbs listed below. Remember to test your verb choice by seeing if you can substitute "is" or "was" for the linking verb.

1. grow   Sentences will vary.
2. has felt
3. seems
4. tasted
5. has remained
6. was

Page 42

Transitive Verbs

A transitive verb is an action verb that is followed by a direct object. The verb "transmits" the action from the subject to the object.
> The teacher graded three papers.

• In each of the following sentences underline the transitive verb and circle the subject and direct object.

1. The fire cast dancing shadows across the room.
2. The choir bought new outfits for the concert.
3. The sleigh rails hit the roof with a loud bang.
4. Rodney handled the flaming torch with ease.
5. The disc jockey picked a song from the list.
6. The outfielder hit the wall with a thud.
7. The goalie stopped the ball.
8. The horse jumped the obstacle with ease.
9. Kenny slugged the baseball into the outfield.
10. He served the tennis ball over the net.
11. The woman painted the room.
12. Charlie washed the windows.
13. My friend types 80 words per minute.
14. The toddler slammed the cupboard drawer on his fingers.

• Write four sentences about a party. Be sure to use transitive verbs. Underline the transitive verbs and circle the direct objects.

1. Sentences will vary.
2.
3.
4.

Page 43

Intransitive Verbs

Name _____

An intransitive verb does not need an object to complete its meaning. It is frequently followed by a prepositional phrase.
The tower underlined{collapsed} to the ground.

• In each of the following sentences, underline the intransitive verb and circle the subject.

1. The (city) of Jerusalem is located near the center of Israel.
2. The (control) of the city of Jerusalem has changed often over the centuries.
3. The (city) was captured by King David.
4. Under his rule the (city) flourished.
5. However, (it) was sacked by the Babylonians in 587 or 586 B.C.
6. The great (Temple of Jerusalem) was built by King Solomon.
7. The (Temple) was destroyed.
8. Jewish (people) gather every day at the Wailing Wall.
9. A (mosque) the Dome of the Rock, was built on the same site.
10. On a nearby site a Christian holy (place) the Church of the Holy Sepulcher, stands.
11. (Jerusalem) is revered by Jews, Christians, and Muslims.
12. Throughout history (tensions) have arisen between the groups.
13. Many (plans) for resolving the disputes have failed.
14. All (signs) in the city are printed in three languages—Hebrew, Arabic, and English.
15. (Pilgrims) come from all over the world to Jerusalem.

• Write five sentences about your city or one that you have visited. Include an intransitive verb in each sentence. Underline the intransitive verbs and circle the subjects.

1. Sentences will vary.
2. _____
3. _____
4. _____
5. _____

Page 44

Simple Tenses

Name _____

The tense of a verb indicates the time an action takes place.
Present tense indicates action or being that is happening now.
Susan underlined{loves} ice cream. She underlined{is} here.
Past tense indicates action or being that was completed in the past.
Matthew underlined{loved} the new movie. He underlined{was} here.
Future tense indicates action or being that will take place in the future. The auxiliary verbs will and shall are used with the principal verb to form the future tense.
Ellen underlined{will love} this house. She underlined{will be} here tomorrow.

• Identify the tense of the verb in each sentence: present tense (P), past tense (PA), or future tense (F). Then rewrite the sentence using another tense.

F 1. I will hike to the top of the mountain.   Sentences will vary.
PA 2. He fought against the onslaught of mosquitoes.
PA 3. Daniel compared this trip to others.
P 4. They wear all the standard gear.
F 5. We shall elect a leader!
PA 6. Naomi was an excellent survivalist.
PA 7. She swept through the underbrush.
F 8. They will collect samples of leaves along the way.
P 9. The groups return to camp each evening.

• Write one sentence in each simple tense about a camping trip.

1. (present) ___ Sentences will vary.
2. (past) _____
3. (future) _____

Page 45

Imperative Mood

Name _____

The mood of the verb indicates the attitude or viewpoint behind the verb's expression. The imperative mood indicates a command or a request. The subject is always "you," though this is rarely expressed.
Please, close the door.
(Notice that "you" is understood to be the subject of this sentence.)

• Use the verbs below to write sentences of your own which are in the imperative mood.

1. check ___ Sentences will vary.
2. return _____
3. wash _____
4. deliver _____
5. develop _____
6. count _____
7. drive _____
8. climb _____
9. send _____
10. take _____
11. stop _____
12. catch _____

• Write three sentences in the imperative mood that you might hear your principal or teacher say. Underline the verbs.

1. Sentences will vary.
2. _____
3. _____

• Put an I by the sentences written in the imperative mood.

____ 1. The boy threw the baseball.   I 5. Pass the paper to me.
I 2. Sit here, please.   ____ 6. I love to paint with watercolors.
____ 3. That movie was thoroughly enjoyable. ____ 7. The windows need to be washed.
I 4. Step up here right now.   I 8. Park the car.

Page 46

Agreement of Subject and Verb

Name _____

A verb must agree with its subject in number. That is, a singular subject requires a singular verb, and a plural subject requires a plural verb.
Singular: The underlined{tree} underlined{sways} in the wind.
Plural: The underlined{trees} underlined{sway} in the wind.
Note: The number of the subject is not changed by a phrase or clause which might follow it.
The underlined{tree} with dozens of coconuts underlined{sways} in the wind.
The underlined{trees} on this island underlined{sway} in the wind.

• Circle the correct verb choice in each of the sentences below.

1. A single lightning bolt (is, are) capable of doing a great deal of damage.
2. The peak temperature of a bolt (heats, heat) the surrounding air to over 60,000°F.
3. The lightning stroke (create, creates) a jagged picture across the sky.
4. Commercial jets (is, are) seldom hit by lightning.
5. If struck, they (suffer, suffers) only slight damage.
6. Planes (has, have) special shielding to protect their electronic equipment.
7. Rocket launches (provide, provides) the best chance to study lightning.
8. Photography (is, are) another way to study lightning.
9. Scientists in many labs (think, thinks) that there is even lightning on Venus.
10. A bolt of lightning from the clouds (is, are) always an awesome sight.

• Write a short paragraph describing what it would be like to be caught out in a boat during a storm. Underline each verb and circle each subject.

Paragraph will vary.

_____
_____
_____
_____
_____

Page 47

© Carson-Dellosa   114   IF8732 Grammar 7–8

Problem Verbs—Lie/Lay

Lie means to recline, to rest, or to remain in a reclining position. The principal parts of the verb *lie* are *lie, lay, (have, has, had) lain*. This verb never takes an object in any of its forms. There is no form of this verb ending in *d. Lie* is sometimes confused with the verb *lay*, which means to put something down or to place something somewhere. Its principal parts are *lay, laid, (have, has, had) laid*. This verb always takes an object.

Examples of sentences using *lie* :
John *lies* down for an hour every day. *present*
John *lay* on the deck in the sun. (not laid) *past*
John *has lain* on the deck often. (not has laid) *past participle*

Examples of sentences using *lay*:
Fred *lays* linoleum for a department store. *present*
Fred *laid* linoleum all day. *past*
Fred *has laid* linoleum since he left high school. *past participle*

- Circle the correct verb in each of the following sentences.

1. He (**lay**, laid) down to take a nap.
2. Lennie has (lain, **laid**) carpet for that store for years.
3. Our dog (laid, **lay**) in the mud.
4. My aunt (lays, **lies**) on the sofa every morning.
5. The hen (**laid**, lay) an egg yesterday morning.
6. The injured animal (**lay**, laid) motionless.
7. I think I will (lay, **lie**) down and take a nap.
8. (**Lay**, Lie) that book down.
9. He had (lain, **laid**) the scissors on the table.

- Use the following verbs in sentences of your own.

1. lies (rests) ___Sentences will vary.___
2. laid (put down) _____
3. lay (reclined) _____

Page 48

Problem Verbs—Sit/Set

The verb *sit* means to assume a sitting position or to occupy a seat. The principal parts of the verb *sit* are *sit, sat, (have, has, had) sat*. The verb *sit* never takes an object. This verb is sometimes confused with the verb *set*, which means to put something in position or to make something rigid. The principal parts of the verb *set* are *set, set, (have, has, had) set*. The verb *set* usually has an object.

Examples of sentences using *sit*:
I sit in the shade whenever I can.
Jack sat still, waiting for the fish to bite.
The governor has sat in that chair for many meetings.

Examples of sentences using *set*:
Tony set the silverware on the table.
Yesterday, Wally set the clock after the storm.
The realtor has set his commission too high.

- Circle the correct verb in each of the following sentences.

1. He (set, **sat**) still while his hair was being cut.
2. You should always (**sit**, set) in good light when you read.
3. Grandpa likes to (**sit**, set) in the rocking chair.
4. We (**set**, sat) the correct time on the computer after the storm ended.
5. The little boy (set, **sat**) there looking depressed.
6. You may (**sit**, set) the book on the table.
7. Please (**sit**, set) here and relax while I try to find your book.
8. Let's (set, **sit**) here and watch the rain.
9. The boys (**sat**, set) on the roof.
10. Paula likes to (**sit**, set) in the easy chair.
11. The doctor (sat, **set**) his leg skillfully.
12. The painter (sat, **set**) his ladders against the building before mixing his paints.

- Use the following verbs in sentences of your own.
1. has set ___Sentences will vary.___
2. sit _____

Page 49

Problem Verbs—Rise/Raise

The verb *rise* means to ascend, to swell up, and to rise in value or force. The principal parts of the verb *rise* are *rise, rose, (have, has, had) risen*. The verb rise does not take an object. This verb is sometimes confused with the verb *raise*, which means to lift up something, to cause it to go up, to increase the amount, to collect a number of objects, or to breed and grow. Its principal parts are *raise, raised, (have, has, had) raised*. The verb *raise* always takes an object.

Examples of sentences using *rise*:
The sun rises in the east.
The rocket rose steadily into the atmosphere.
The tide had risen by morning.

Examples of sentences using *raise*:
Many farmers raise soybeans as a cash crop.
Sheila raised the flag.
The charismatic politician had raised a huge sum of money.

- Circle the correct verb in each of the following sentences.

1. The hot air balloon (raises, **rises**) into the blue sky.
2. The stock market (**rose**, raised) 30 points yesterday because of the President's announcement.
3. The granite cliffs (raise, **rise**) high above the valley.
4. The guerilla leader (**raised**, rose) a great army of support.
5. The flood waters (raised, **rose**) rapidly.
6. The coffee dealers (rose, **raised**) the price of coffee beans.
7. The soldier (rose, **raised**) the flag.
8. The wedding guests had (**raised**, risen) their glasses to sip champagne for a toast.

- Use the verbs below to write sentences of your own.
1. raise ___Sentences will vary.___
2. rises _____
3. rose _____
4. had raised _____

Page 50

Troublesome Verbs

- Fill in the missing principal parts of the irregular verbs in the chart.

Present Tense	Past Tense	Past Participle
shake	shook	(have, has, had) shaken
lead	**led**	(have, has, had) led
freeze	froze	(have, has, had) **frozen**
eat	**ate**	(have, has, had) eaten
wear	**wore**	(have, has, had) worn
know	knew	(have, has, had) **known**
blow	**blew**	(have, has, had) blown
drown	drowned	(have, has, had) drowned
catch	caught	(have, has, had) **caught**

- Circle the correct verb in each of the following sentences.

1. Kendra (blow, **blew**) out the candles on her birthday cake.
2. You have (ate, **eaten**) all of the treats put out for the party.
3. What will you (**wear**, have worn) to the party tomorrow?
4. John (**shook**, shaked) his head.
5. I (**knew**, knowed) it was his birthday.
6. He almost (**drowned**, drownded) trying to bob for apples.
7. I did not know to where the path (leaded, **led**).
8. The pond has been (froze, **frozen**) for several weeks now.
9. Terry (catched, **caught**) a cold the day before the party.
10. I have (weared, **worn**) this dress before.
11. After an hour outside, the water in the pail had (**frozen**, froze).

- Use the verbs below to write sentences of your own.
1. ate ___Sentences will vary.___
2. lead _____
3. have shaken _____

Page 51

More Troublesome Verbs

• Fill in the missing principal parts of the irregular verbs in the chart.

Present Tense	Past Tense	Past Participle
become	became	(have, has, had) become
choose	chose	(have, has, had) chosen
drink	drank	(have, has, had) drunk
throw	threw	(have, has, had) thrown
write	wrote	(have, has, had) written
flow	flowed	(have, has, had) flowed
see	saw	(have, has, had) seen
swear	swore	(have, has, had) sworn
climb	climbed	(have, has, had) climbed

• Circle the correct verb choices in the following sentences.

1. Roger has (swore, **sworn**) to tell the truth.
2. The rising river (**flowed**, flew) under the bridge.
3. Ursula (**wrote**, written) many interesting letters.
4. Sam (become, **became**) angry yesterday.
5. Paul (**has**, have) climbed that tree in the backyard many times.
6. He (**saw**, seen) that movie three times already.
7. I have (choosed, **chosen**) Michael to be on our team.
8. I (drunk, **drank**) all my milk, Mom!
9. The boy had (threw, **thrown**) the ball into the woods.
10. The knight (sweared, **swore**) his loyalty to the king.
11. Sara has (became, **become**) a wonderful cook.
12. We found that the juice had (flew, **flowed**) from the hole in the cup.

• Use the verbs below to write sentences of your own.

1. has seen ___Sentences will vary.___
2. have written _____
3. have thrown _____

Page 52

And More Troublesome Verbs

• Fill in the missing principal parts of the irregular verbs in the chart.

Present Tense	Past Tense	Past Participle
cut	cut	(have, has, had) cut
drag	dragged	(have, has, had) dragged
wring	wrung	(have, has, had) wrung
weave	wove	(have, has, had) woven
lend	lent	(have, has, had) lent
say	said	(have, has, had) said
take	took	(have, has, had) taken
let	let	(have, has, had) let
go	went	(have, has, had) gone

• Circle the correct verb in each of the following sentences.

1. She has (wove, **woven**) a beautiful pattern into that garment.
2. Harris (**lent**, lended) Jake a lot of money.
3. Bob (say, **said**) that he is not going to the game.
4. This whole thing has (**taken**, took) far too long already.
5. Ellen (**wrung**, wringed) the water from the rag.
6. Grandpa (**went**, gone) to the store yesterday.
7. Sara had (**cut**, cutted) the cake and grabbed a piece before anyone noticed.
8. We have (went, **gone**) to that restaurant before.
9. The gardener (drug, **dragged**) the heavy shrub to the truck.

• Use the verbs below to write sentences of your own.

1. have gone ___Sentences will vary.___
2. let _____
3. has lent _____
4. wrung _____
5. had said _____

Page 53

Persons of Pronouns

The person of a pronoun tells whether the pronoun being used is the speaker, the one spoken to, or the one spoken about.
— The first person refers to the one speaking.
  I am speaking.
— The second person refers to the one spoken to.
  You are the one.
— The third person refers to the person or thing spoken about.
  She/It is beautiful.

• In each of the following sentences, identify the person of each underlined pronoun by writing 1, 2, or 3 in the parentheses at the end of each sentence.

1. He was a soldier in the Civil War. (**3**)
2. I would like you to study the chapter on the causes of the war. (**2**)
3. We must understand the problems left behind at the end of the war. (**1**)
4. Abraham Lincoln guided it through a very difficult time. (**3**)
5. I admire Ulysses S. Grant. (**1**)
6. He was a talented general. (**3**)
7. The war created many problems, but it also solved a most serious one—slavery. (**3**)
8. Have you studied the Civil War before? (**2**)
9. My history teacher was correct when she said this material was important to learn. (**3**)
10. We will soon learn a poem written during this time. (**1**)

• Circle each first person pronoun, underline each second person pronoun, and draw a rectangle around each third person pronoun.

(I)   [he]   she   you   (we)   [it]

• Write one sentence using first person, one sentence using second person, and one using third person. Circle the pronouns which indicate the person.

1. (first person) ___Sentences will vary.___
2. (second person) _____
3. (third person) _____

Page 54

Personal Pronouns

A pronoun is a word that takes the place of a noun. A *personal pronoun* indicates the speaker (first person), the one spoken to (second person), or the one spoken about (third person).
First person pronouns: I, my, mine, me, we, our, ours, us
Second person pronouns: you, your, yours
Third person pronouns: he, she, it, his, her, hers, its, him, her, they, their, theirs, them

• Place a number 1 above first person pronouns, a 2 above second person pronouns, and a 3 above third person pronouns in the following sentences.

1. We are going to study the life of Joan of Arc.
2. What do you think we will learn from this study?
3. When Joan of Arc was thirteen years old, she realized her life was going to change.
4. She became convinced that Charles VII, the King of France, needed her help to drive out the English soldiers.
5. If you had been there, you might have doubted Joan's ability to help.
6. When she was seventeen she finally talked to the king.
7. Joan had talked to a commander first, and he laughed at her.
8. They did not think she would be of any help.
9. She led them in battle and was victorious at the Battle of Orléans.
10. Eventually she was captured and held prisoner by the English.
11. They thought she was a witch and burned her at the stake on May 30, 1431.
12. We will probably never know all of the details of her exciting life.
13. Do you admire her?
14. I do admire her bravery.

• Write three sentences about a daring adventure on which you would like to embark. Use at least one personal pronoun in each sentence. Underline the personal pronouns.

1. ___Sentences will vary.___
2. _____
3. _____

Page 55

Number and Gender of Pronouns

A pronoun must agree with its antecedent (the noun it refers to) in number and gender. If the noun is singular, the pronoun must be singular. If the noun is plural, the pronoun must be plural. If the noun is masculine, the pronoun must be masculine. If the noun is feminine, the pronoun must be feminine. If the noun is neuter (neither sex indicated), the pronoun must also be neuter.

• In the following sentences, place an **S** under the pronouns that are singular and a **P** under those that are plural. Then put an **F** above the pronouns that are female, an **M** above those that are male, and an **N** above those that are neuter.

1. Mary is the first person I would invite to the party. She is fun to talk to.

2. The car veered to the left of the line. It then stopped suddenly.

3. Can you go to the mall with Sara and me? We are leaving at 1:00 P.M.

4. We slid down the water slide. It was a very fast ride.

5. Tony's idea of a good time is to sit in front of the TV all night. He doesn't even like to play basketball.

6. We saw the plane heading toward the airport. Dad and I both checked the time to see if it was late.

7. The pilot let Billy sit in the cockpit. Boy was he thrilled!

8. Have you ever flown on a plane? Would you like to fly?

• Write a pronoun to take the place of the following nouns.

1. shelter	it	6. mountain	it
2. soccer	it	7. bull	it
3. relatives	they / them	8. daffodils	they / them
4. men	they / them	9. trains	they / them
5. dolphins	they / them	10. ewe	it

Page 56

Indefinite Pronouns

An indefinite pronoun is one which refers generally, not specifically, to persons, places, or things. Some indefinite pronouns are always singular, some are always plural, and some may be either singular or plural.

Singular indefinite pronouns: anybody, anyone, another, each, either, everybody, everyone, nobody, no one, neither, one, other, someone, somebody, everything, anything, something

Plural indefinite pronouns: many, both, few, several, others

Indefinite pronouns that may be either singular or plural: all, any, most, some, none

Remember: The number of the subject of the sentence is not affected by any phrases or clauses that come between it and the verb.

• In each of the following sentences, circle the verb or helping verb that agrees in number with the indefinite pronoun subject.

1. Every one of the students (like, likes) to be challenged.
2. Some of the material in this book (is, are) interesting.
3. Either of the two sisters (is, are) willing to pay for the gift.
4. Many of the people (was, were) disgusted with the media coverage.
5. Neither of the two teams (deserve, deserves) to play in the finals.
6. Anyone who thinks they know the answer (has, have) to raise his or her hand.
7. Each of the monkeys in the cage (play, plays) to the audience.
8. Most of the rocks in the bag (is, are) worthless.
9. All of the fish in the creek (was, were) killed by the insecticide.
10. Everyone who is interested (is, are) welcome to sign up.
11. Everybody in the band (is, are) very talented.
12. All of us (wish, wishes) the best for your future.
13. Several of the women on the job site (was, were) given a raise.
14. Few teachers (has, have) been as energetic as she has been.
15. One elephant (has, have) done a tremendous amount of damage to the village.

Page 57

Possessive and Interrogative Pronouns

A possessive pronoun is one which indicates ownership or possession.
Possessive pronouns: my, mine, your, yours, his, her, hers, its, our, ours, their, theirs

• Circle the possessive pronouns in the following sentences.

1. Her vacation was planned a long time in advance.
2. My travel agent helped put together her itinerary.
3. His office telephoned many hotels and motels around the country.
4. He was asking about their best rate.
5. One hotel sent a brochure of its services.
6. He drove their van to the airport.
7. Our airport is open all night.
8. Is that suitcase hers?
9. Those boxes are theirs.
10. Our flight is delayed.

An interrogative pronoun introduces a question.
Interrogative pronouns: who, whom, whose, what, which

• Circle the interrogative pronoun in each of the following sentences.

1. Who will win this game tonight?
2. Which is your house?
3. What are we having for dinner?
4. To whom will the people of this country turn?
5. Whose child is this?

• Use the following interrogative pronouns to write sentences of your own.

1. what _____ Sentences will vary.
2. which _____
3. whose _____
4. who _____
5. whom _____

Page 58

Reflexive and Relative Pronouns

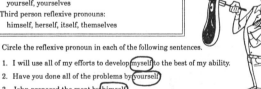

Reflexive pronouns are formed by adding *-self* or *-selves* to certain forms of personal pronouns.
First person reflexive pronouns:
   myself, ourselves
Second person reflexive pronouns:
   yourself, yourselves
Third person reflexive pronouns:
   himself, herself, itself, themselves

• Circle the reflexive pronoun in each of the following sentences.

1. I will use all of my efforts to develop myself to the best of my ability.
2. Have you done all of the problems by yourself?
3. John prepared the meat by himself.
4. We must defend ourselves because no one else will.
5. You might find yourselves needing help one day.
6. Rachael knew herself well enough to know when to ask for help.
7. She watched herself on TV and felt foolish.

Relative pronouns are used to introduce groups of words that act as adjectives.
Relative pronouns: who, whose, whom, which, that

• Circle the relative pronouns.

1. A breakfast that includes fruit is often recommended by nutritionists.
2. People who eat a good breakfast are full of energy in the late morning hours.
3. The dietician in whom I have put my trust is planning my meals.
4. She showed me a low-fat diet that I must follow.
5. She is a person who always eats healthy foods.
6. The diet which I started last night, is easy to follow.
7. My sister who is very slender, can eat whatever she wants.
8. She can't understand a person like me who has to watch everything I eat.

Page 59

IF8732 Grammar 7–8

Subject and Object Pronouns

Name _____

> When a pronoun is the subject of the sentence, it is called a **subject pronoun**.
> He caught the ball. (subject)
> When a pronoun is used as the direct object, indirect object, or object of a preposition, it is called an **object pronoun**.
> Sally saw us. (direct object)
> Matthew throws us the balls. (indirect object)
> Todd threw the ball to us. (object of preposition)

• Circle the pronouns used as subjects, and underline the pronouns used as objects.

1. (We) will never allow it to happen in this school.
2. After thinking about it carefully, (he) decided to go anyway.
3. Even though the fruit was spoiled, the grocer sold it at the same price.
4. (They) told us that this was going to be a very exciting day.
5. (I) decided how the money should be spent.
6. (I) wanted her to help me make the decision.
7. (She) refused to do this.
8. Harry wanted to buy it at the fruit stand.
9. (They) did not stock apricot jam there.
10. (He) told them about a grocery store located several blocks away.
11. Mark told me about a movie.
12. (We) chatted about it while walking to the store.

• Write a short paragraph about a visit to another country using at least three subject pronouns and three object pronouns.

_____ *Paragraph will vary.* _____

Page 60

Pronouns Who/Whom

Name _____

> The use of the pronouns *who* and *whom* is determined by the pronoun's function in the clause. Generally, *who* is used as a subject of a sentence or clause.
> <u>Who</u> baked the cake?
> The boy <u>who</u> baked it lives next door to me.
> **Whom** is used as a direct object or an object of a preposition.
> <u>Whom</u> did you visit last week?
> With <u>whom</u> did you travel?

• Circle the correct pronoun in each of the following sentences.

1. Mr. Hands is the one (who, whom) handles disciplinary matters.
2. Do you think he is one in (who, whom) you can put your trust?
3. Matthew is well acquainted with people (who, whom) will tell the truth.
4. Kent is the person with (who, whom) you should speak.
5. (Who, Whom) is waiting for me?
6. For (who, whom) do you think we should vote?
7. To (who, whom) do you wish to speak?
8. The girl (who, whom) we met is very intelligent.
9. Phyllis, (who, whom) is my youngest sister, is going to become a doctor.
10. The person to (who, whom) you spoke is no longer here.
11. (Who, Whom) went to the play?
12. With (who, whom) did you see the movie?
13. My brother, (who, whom) lives in Georgia, likes to jog.
14. (Who, Whom) is coming to the party?

• Using the pronouns **who** and **whom**, write a short paragraph about something that you have studied in American history.

_____ *Paragraph will vary.* _____

Page 61

Sentences with Modifiers

Name _____

> The complete subject or complete predicate of a sentence usually contains other words or phrases called **modifiers** that add to the meaning of the sentence.
> The <u>cold</u> water dripped <u>slowly over the jagged edge</u>.

• In the following sentences, underline the subject modifiers once and the predicate modifiers twice.

1. The small boy ran very fast.
2. The huge, gray dog ran eagerly.
3. The talented magician bowed gracefully.
4. The distraught mother silently watched.
5. The excited boy collided with the dog.
6. The long-stemmed roses landed in a tangled mess on the floor.
7. The frightened cat in the window jumped wildly.

• Add modifiers to the simple subjects and predicates below and create interesting sentences. Don't forget to capitalize the first word of the sentence.

1. player won game _____ *Sentences will vary.*
2. car drove _____
3. children played _____
4. birds flew _____
5. Michelangelo painted murals _____
6. Miss Brown explained problem _____
7. sun shines _____
8. summer means _____
9. lakes freeze _____
10. trees grow _____

Page 62

Identifying Adjectives

Name _____

> An **adjective** modifies a noun or pronoun. It gives specific information by telling *what kind, how many,* or *which one.*
> green grass, two swimmers, this book

• In each of the following sentences, underline the adjective(s). Then tell what question each answers by writing a number above it: **1**—what kind? **2**—how many? **3**—which one(s)?

1. Ralph took his mangy, old dog for a long walk.
2. The dog, Joshua, reluctantly rose from the warm bricks in front of the blazing hearth.
3. He did not understand why anyone would want to venture out into the cold weather.
4. Ralph wore his bright red stocking cap pulled tightly over his big ears.
5. The cold air stung his red nose as he slogged through the blinding snow.
6. Those majestic pines were covered with a heavy layer of snow.
7. Joshua immediately had tiny icicles form in the fur of his four paws.
8. He stopped two times to try to remove the icy buildup.
9. When Ralph saw the pitiful look on Joshua's face, he knew he had made a mistake.
10. That dog endured the bitter wind.
11. He turned back to the warm house they had just left.
12. Joshua raced ahead to get back to the safe haven of his peaceful, toasty hearth.
13. Ralph peeled off the several layers of thick wool clothes and sat by the roaring fire.
14. He decided that the next time he took a long walk it would be a warm, spring day.
15. The faithful dog wagged his bushy tail.

• Write four sentences of your own using at least one adjective in each. Write about a summer day. Underline the adjectives.

1. _____ *Sentences will vary.*
2. _____
3. _____
4. _____

Page 63

© Carson-Dellosa   118   IF8732 Grammar 7–8

Descriptive Adjectives

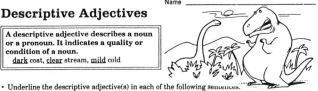

> A descriptive adjective describes a noun or a pronoun. It indicates a quality or condition of a noun.
> <u>dark</u> coat, <u>clear</u> stream, <u>mild</u> cold

- Underline the descriptive adjective(s) in each of the following sentences.

1. The dinosaurs were the <u>dominant</u> <u>land</u> animal 65 million years ago.
2. The name was derived from a <u>Greek</u> word meaning "<u>terrible</u> lizard."
3. These animals reached <u>gigantic</u> proportions.
4. A <u>large</u> number of dinosaurs were <u>flesh</u> eaters.
5. Some dinosaurs abandoned this diet for a <u>herbivorous</u> diet.
6. The <u>earlier</u> and more <u>primitive</u> types were actually <u>small</u>, <u>reptile-like</u> animals.
7. Suddenly the record of the <u>huge</u> monsters stops.
8. How do we explain this <u>sudden</u> extinction?
9. One theory blames <u>temperature</u> changes.
10. Another theory suggests that <u>geological</u> changes occurred which reduced <u>food</u> sources.
11. Many <u>thrilling</u> movies revolve around these <u>amazing</u> reptiles.
12. Kids all over the world would miss hearing <u>blood-curdling</u> screams in their <u>favorite</u> <u>dinosaur</u> movies.
13. <u>Nervous</u> children would not have to ask for their <u>special</u> <u>night</u> light.
14. <u>Brave</u> parents wouldn't have to search the <u>dark</u> driveway for <u>mysterious</u>, <u>scaly</u> prowlers.
15. Could you write an <u>exciting</u> book about these <u>incredible</u> creatures?

- Write five sentences about dinosaurs using at least one descriptive adjective in each. Underline the descriptive adjectives.

1. _Sentences will vary._
2. _____
3. _____
4. _____
5. _____

Comparative Degree of Adjectives

> The comparative degree of an adjective is used when showing a comparison between two persons or things. It shows a greater or lesser degree of quality.
> Almost every adjective of one syllable forms its comparative degree by adding -er.
> stronger, neater, warmer
> An adjective with two or more syllables forms its comparative degree by adding *more* or *less* in front of the adjective.
> more clever, less difficult
> An adjective of one syllable that ends in *y* usually forms its comparative degree by changing the *y* to *i* and adding -er.
> handier, clumsier

- In each of the following sentences, underline the adjective in the comparative degree.

1. It was a <u>stormier</u> night than usual at our cottage.
2. First there was a <u>harder</u> rain than we were used to seeing.
3. This was followed by <u>stronger</u> winds than we experience at home.
4. If the roof had been <u>flimsier</u>, it would have blown away.
5. But the roof was <u>more sturdy</u> than we thought.
6. I can't imagine a <u>more dismal</u> evening.
7. Large hailstones started to fall, followed by even <u>larger</u> ones.
8. My sister, who is <u>younger</u> than I am, was scared.
9. We heard a clap of thunder which was <u>louder</u> than an explosion.
10. The next day brought a <u>calmer</u> sky.

- Write four sentences of your own with each including at least one adjective in the comparative degree. Underline the comparative adjectives.

1. _Sentences will vary._
2. _____
3. _____
4. _____

Superlative Degree of Adjectives

> The superlative degree of an adjective is used when more than two persons or things are being compared. It indicates that the quality is possessed to the greatest or least degree by one of the persons or things being compared.
> Adjectives of one syllable usually form the superlative degree by adding -est.
> strongest, neatest, warmest
> An adjective of two or more syllables forms the superlative degree by adding *most* or *least* in front of the adjective.
> most clever, least difficult
> An adjective of one syllable that ends in *y* usually forms the superlative degree by changing the *y* to *i* and adding -est.
> handiest, clumsiest

- In the following sentences, underline the adjectives that are in the superlative degree.

1. That was the <u>greatest</u> movie I ever saw!
2. It had the <u>most glamorous</u> stars in the most exotic settings imaginable.
3. Even though the story was one of the <u>tallest</u> tales I've heard, I still enjoyed it.
4. The hero had to perform the <u>most difficult</u> stunts of all.
5. The special effects were the <u>most intricate</u> ever attempted.
6. The part of the heroine was played by the <u>most talented</u> actress in the world.
7. The villain was the <u>nastiest</u> character they could have found for the part.
8. The <u>weakest</u> part of the film was the ending.
9. It seems they selected the <u>silliest</u> conclusion possible.

- Write four sentences of your own about a movie you have seen. Each sentence should include at least one adjective in the superlative degree. Underline the superlative degree adjectives.

1. _Sentences will vary._
2. _____
3. _____
4. _____

Irregular Comparison of Adjectives

> Some adjectives have an irregular form of comparison. An irregular adjective forms the degree of comparison by a complete change in the word itself.

Note: Study the forms below before attempting the activity. Always consult a dictionary if you are in doubt about which form to use.

Positive	Comparative	Superlative
much	more	most
bad	worse	worst
good	better	best
far	farther	farthest
little	less	least

- In each of the following sentences, underline the irregular form of the adjective.

1. That was the <u>best</u> meal he has ever cooked.
2. He won a prize at the reunion because he drove a <u>farther</u> distance than anyone else.
3. Hank said he had a <u>better</u> day today than he had yesterday.
4. That is the <u>worst</u> poem I have ever read.
5. That is the <u>most</u> homework the class has ever been given.
6. The hungry girl ate <u>less</u> ham than eggs.
7. Of all the chefs, he added the <u>least</u> salt to his chili.

> There are some adjectives that should not be compared because the positive degree is already the highest possible degree. For example, if something is *empty* it cannot be *emptier*.
> **Examples:** empty, correct, perfect, final, full, alone, wrong, supreme, single

- Use the following adjectives to write sentences of your own.

1. correct _Sentences will vary._
2. final _____
3. perfect _____

Limiting Adjectives

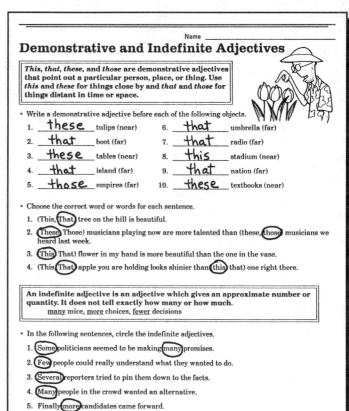

A limiting adjective is one that points out an object or indicates its number or quantity. The articles *a*, *an*, and *the* are limiting adjectives. *A* precedes a noun beginning with a consonant sound, and *an* precedes a noun beginning with a vowel sound.

the cat, a dog, an owl, an hour

• Write *a* or *an* in front of each noun.

1. _a_ garage 5. _an_ ant 9. _an_ honor 13. _a_ car
2. _a_ CD 6. _a_ baseball 10. _a_ sale 14. _an_ uncle
3. _an_ apple 7. _an_ order 11. _an_ elevator 15. _a_ carpet
4. _a_ disaster 8. _a_ concert 12. _a_ video 16. _a_ floor

A numerical adjective is a limiting adjective that indicates an exact number.
one, thirty, fifty

• In the following sentences, circle the articles and underline the numerical adjectives.

1. (The) top speed limit on (the) interstate expressway is fifty-five miles per hour.
2. (A) two-hundred dollar fine may result if you speed.
3. There are only about five cars that pass this point every day.
4. Twenty police officers have been assigned to monitor (the) city streets.
5. If they save just one life, it will be worth (the) effort.
6. (The) traffic laws review book contained twenty-three pages.
7. I read (the) book ten times.

• Write sentences of your own about driving a car. Use a numerical adjective in each sentence.

1. Sentences will vary.
2.
3.
4.
5.

Page 68

Demonstrative and Indefinite Adjectives

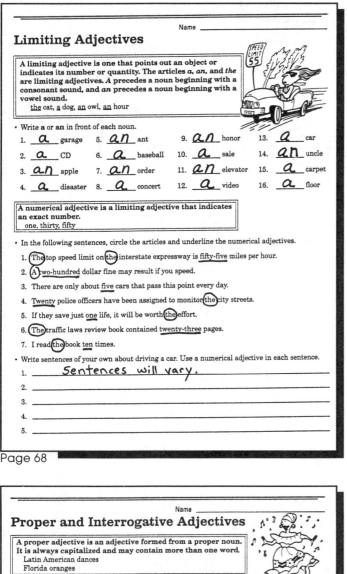

This, *that*, *these*, and *those* are demonstrative adjectives that point out a particular person, place, or thing. Use *this* and *these* for things close by and *that* and *those* for things distant in time or space.

• Write a demonstrative adjective before each of the following objects.

1. these tulips (near) 6. that umbrella (far)
2. that boot (far) 7. that radio (far)
3. these tables (near) 8. this stadium (near)
4. that island (far) 9. that nation (far)
5. those empires (far) 10. these textbooks (near)

• Choose the correct word or words for each sentence.

1. (This, (That)) tree on the hill is beautiful.
2. ((These) Those) musicians playing now are more talented than (these, (those)) musicians we heard last week.
3. ((This) That) flower in my hand is more beautiful than the one in the vase.
4. (This, (That)) apple you are holding looks shinier than ((this) that) one right there.

An indefinite adjective is an adjective which gives an approximate number or quantity. It does not tell exactly how many or how much.
many mice, more choices, fewer decisions

• In the following sentences, circle the indefinite adjectives.

1. (Some) politicians seemed to be making (many) promises.
2. (Few) people could really understand what they wanted to do.
3. (Several) reporters tried to pin them down to the facts.
4. (Many) people in the crowd wanted an alternative.
5. Finally (more) candidates came forward.
6. They talked like they understood (many) problems.
7. (All) people could support these candidates.

Page 69

Proper and Interrogative Adjectives

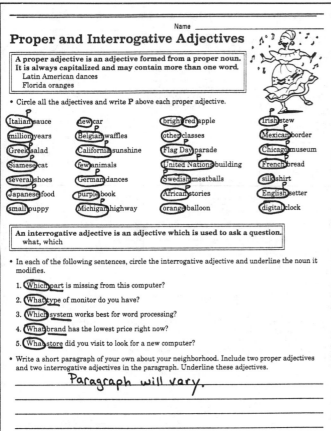

A proper adjective is an adjective formed from a proper noun. It is always capitalized and may contain more than one word.
Latin American dances
Florida oranges

• Circle all the adjectives and write **P** above each proper adjective.

(Italian) sauce (new) car (bright red) apple (Irish) stew
(million) years (Belgian) waffles (other) classes (Mexican) border
(Greek) salad (California) sunshine (Flag Day) parade (Chicago) museum
(Siamese) cat (few) animals (United Nations) building (French) bread
(several) shoes (German) dances (Swedish) meatballs (silk) shirt
(Japanese) food (purple) book (African) stories (English) setter
(small) puppy (Michigan) highway (orange) balloon (digital) clock

An interrogative adjective is an adjective which is used to ask a question.
what, which

• In each of the following sentences, circle the interrogative adjective and underline the noun it modifies.

1. (Which) part is missing from this computer?
2. (What) type of monitor do you have?
3. (Which) system works best for word processing?
4. (What) brand has the lowest price right now?
5. (What) store did you visit to look for a new computer?

• Write a short paragraph of your own about your neighborhood. Include two proper adjectives and two interrogative adjectives in the paragraph. Underline these adjectives.

Paragraph will vary.

Page 70

Predicate Adjectives

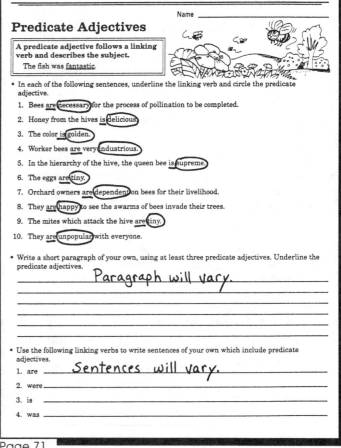

A predicate adjective follows a linking verb and describes the subject.
The fish was fantastic.

• In each of the following sentences, underline the linking verb and circle the predicate adjective.

1. Bees are (necessary) for the process of pollination to be completed.
2. Honey from the hives is (delicious).
3. The color is (golden).
4. Worker bees are very (industrious).
5. In the hierarchy of the hive, the queen bee is (supreme).
6. The eggs are (tiny).
7. Orchard owners are (dependent) on bees for their livelihood.
8. They are (happy) to see the swarms of bees invade their trees.
9. The mites which attack the hive are (tiny).
10. They are (unpopular) with everyone.

• Write a short paragraph of your own, using at least three predicate adjectives. Underline the predicate adjectives.

Paragraph will vary.

• Use the following linking verbs to write sentences of your own which include predicate adjectives.

1. are Sentences will vary.
2. were
3. is
4. was

Page 71

120

IF8732 Grammar 7–8

Adverbs of Time

> An adverb is a word that modifies a verb, an adjective, or another adverb. Adverbs indicate time, place, or manner. **Adverbs of time** answer the question *when* or *how often.* They usually modify verbs.
> People <u>seldom</u> like to be given orders.

- In the following sentences, circle the adverbs of time and underline the verbs they modify.

1. People <u>have</u> (always) <u>needed</u> some form of government.
2. (First) <u>came</u> dictatorships of one form or another.
3. (Then) the king or dictator <u>made</u> all of the decisions.
4. (Eventually) the ancient Greeks <u>established</u> a form of government they called democracy.
5. It was called democracy, but the people who did not own land <u>could</u> (never) <u>vote.</u>
6. (Later) the Romans <u>adapted</u> this system into a republican form of government.
7. Under this system, the results <u>were</u> (often) representative of the people's wishes.
8. This form was always better than the totalitarian forms which (eventually) <u>followed.</u>
9. Totalitarian governments (frequently) <u>allow</u> human rights abuses.
10. (Today) people around the world <u>look</u> to the United States as a model of democracy.
11. They (often) <u>feel</u> that the democratic system works better than any other that <u>has been</u> <u>tried</u> (before)
12. Even Americans <u>are</u> (constantly) working to improve their democratic system.
13. There <u>is</u> (always) room for improvement in any system.

- Use the following adverbs of time to write sentences of your own about a historical event you have studied recently. Underline the verbs that are being modified.

1. finally _____ Sentences will vary. _____
2. seldom _____
3. already _____
4. frequently _____
5. often _____
6. usually _____

Adverbs of Place

> **Adverbs of place** answer the question *where.* They usually modify verbs.
> The fish swam <u>below</u>.

- In the following sentences, circle the adverbs of place and underline the verbs they modify.

1. People <u>have looked</u> (everywhere) for a satisfactory type of government.
2. The Japanese <u>stayed</u> (away) from the democratic style.
3. They preferred a government system which <u>developed</u> (nearby.)
4. Back in the mid 600s, an emperor <u>ruled</u> (there.)
5. Sailors <u>came</u> (here) from Europe in 1543.
6. Japan <u>focused</u> (inward) during the 1630s.
7. In 1854, Commodore Perry <u>brought</u> (in) U.S. trade.
8. By 1868, the emperor <u>looked</u> (outside) for ideas to modernize Japan.
9. This technology <u>spread</u> (out) from the leaders to the people.
10. Today, many Western nations <u>look</u> (there) for ways to improve their own economies.

- Write a short paragraph using three adverbs of place. Circle the adverbs of place and underline the verbs they modify.

Paragraph will vary. _____

- Use the following adverbs of place to write sentences of your own. Underline the verbs they modify.

1. underneath _____ Sentences will vary. _____
2. away _____
3. inside _____
4. downward _____

Adverbs of Manner

> **Adverbs of manner** answer the question *how* or *in what manner.* They usually end in *-ly.*
> Do your work <u>thoroughly</u>.

- In the following sentences, circle the adverbs of manner and underline the verbs they modify.

1. People all over the world (eagerly) <u>play</u> association football, known here as soccer.
2. Beginners must <u>listen</u> (carefully) to understand the rules.
3. When they <u>understand</u> (completely) they will be ready to play the game.
4. The round ball must <u>be</u> (carefully) controlled.
5. Soccer can (easily) <u>be played</u> almost anywhere.
6. It is exciting to watch players (gracefully) <u>execute</u> complex foot movements.
7. Fans <u>react</u> (emotionally) when their favorite team loses.
8. The game <u>was</u> first <u>played</u> (competitively) in Great Britain in the late 1800s.
9. Games like soccer were <u>played</u> (passionately) by the Chinese in the third century B.C.
10. Soccer <u>spread</u> (rapidly) from Great Britain throughout the world.
11. The World Cup, soccer's championship, is the most (avidly) <u>watched</u> soccer game in the world.
12. The United States <u>has</u> (slowly) <u>begun</u> to accept soccer.
13. Americans found out that it is a game that <u>must be played</u> (intensely.)
14. Someday, perhaps when the U.S. wins the World Cup, soccer <u>will be taken</u> (seriously) in this country.
15. Until then, U.S. fans <u>will watch</u> (hopefully) as other countries dominate the game.

- Write five sentences about a sport you like to play using an adverb of manner in each. Circle the adverbs of manner and underline the verbs that they modify.

1. _____ Sentences will vary. _____
2. _____
3. _____
4. _____
5. _____

Comparison of Adverbs

> Like adjectives, many adverbs also have degrees of comparison. The three degrees of comparison are positive, comparative, and superlative. Some adverbs form the comparative degree by adding *-er* and the superlative degree by adding *-est.* Most adverbs that end in *-ly* form their comparative degrees by adding the word *more* or *less* infront of the positive degree. The superlative degree is formed by adding the word *most* or *least* in front of the positive degree.

- Complete the missing adverbs in the chart.

Positive	Comparative	Superlative
fast	faster	fastest
carefully	more/less carefully	most/least carefully
soon	sooner	soonest
hard	harder	hardest
noisily	more/less noisily	most/least noisily
late	later	latest
easily	more/less easily	most/least easily
efficiently	more/less efficiently	most/least efficiently
loudly	more/less loudly	most/least loudly
proudly	more/less proudly	most/least proudly
harshly	more/less harshly	most/least harshly
neatly	more/less neatly	most/least neatly
cheerfully	more/less cheerfully	most/least cheerfully
courageously	more/less courageously	most/least courageously
highly	more/less highly	most/least highly

- In the following sentences circle the adverbs and indicate the degree of comparison. (**P**—positive, **C**—comparative, **S**—superlative)

C 1. In order to be a good goalie, you have to reach (more quickly) than the average person.
P 2. The puck slides across the ice (fast.)
S 3. The teammate skating (nearest) will help you fend off the attack.
P 4. You might be pushed (roughly) onto the ice.
C 5. When a player has the puck, watch him or her (more carefully.)
S 6. The player who guides the puck (most skillfully) makes many goals.
C 7. A good player is (less easily) discouraged than you would think.
S 8. That player gets back on the ice (most quickly.)

Adverbs and Adjectives

When trying to determine whether to use an adjective or an adverb, decide which word is being modified. Adjectives modify nouns and pronouns. Adverbs modify verbs, adjectives, and other adverbs.

• In the following sentences, circle the correct word. Then identify it by writing **ADV** (adverb) or **ADJ** (adjective) in the blank.

ADV 1. The sound track began very (strange, (strangely))

ADJ 2. There was a ((sudden) suddenly) surge of volume.

ADV 3. This was followed by an announcer (calm, (calmly)) announcing the names of the cast.

ADJ 4. It is not the ((usual) usually) way for a film to begin.

ADV 5. The credits were (extreme, (extremely)) long.

ADV 6. We were (true, (truly)) in for a different experience.

ADV 7. (Gradual, (Gradually)) the actual movie started.

ADJ 8. I had been ((wise) wisely) to go out for popcorn during the credits.

ADJ 9. But I felt ((guilty) guiltily) because I didn't bring my sister any.

ADV 10. The plot moved (swift, (swiftly)) into a series of wild chases.

ADV 11. Each one was performed more (awkward, (awkwardly)) than the last.

ADJ 12. The actors' performances were very ((poor) poorly).

ADJ 13. I can't remember when I saw a more ((odd) oddly) movie.

ADV 14. I couldn't get out of there (quick, (quickly)) enough.

ADV 15. Next time, I'm going to read the review more (thorough, (thoroughly)).

• Use the following adjectives and adverbs in sentences of your own. Circle the modifiers and underline the words being modified.

1. clever _Sentences will vary._
2. gradually _____
3. honest _____
4. genuinely _____
5. happily _____
6. great _____

Double Negatives

A double negative is an incorrect construction that uses two negative words when one is sufficient. Use only one negative word when you mean "no."
Incorrect: He did <u>not</u> do <u>nothing</u> all day. (two negative words)
Correct: He did <u>not</u> do anything all day. (or) He did <u>nothing</u> all day. (one negative word)

• Circle the negative words in the following sentences. Then rewrite each sentence so that it does not contain a double negative construction.

1. I haven't got no time to wait for you.   _Sentences will vary._
2. You don't know nothing about the subject we're discussing. _____
3. You can't hardly find that tape anywhere. _____
4. Oprah said that she didn't want no one on the show with his attitude. _____
5. David couldn't hardly believe his good luck. _____
6. My brother doesn't do nothing all day long. _____
7. Gerald hasn't never been to New York City before. _____
8. The police told the press that they would not have no further statements until Monday. _____
9. Polly didn't have nowhere to go, so she pouted. _____
10. All of this work doesn't scarcely leave time for me to play. _____

• Use the negative words below to write sentences of your own about safety rules.

1. never _Sentences will vary._
2. nothing _____
3. could not _____
4. no _____
5. have not _____

Adjective Prepositional Phrases

A prepositional phrase is a group of words that shows how two words or ideas are related to each other. It can function as an adjective or an adverb depending on the word it modifies. Like a one-word adjective, an adjective prepositional phrase modifies a noun or pronoun.
The shady ground <u>under the elm tree</u> was perfect.

• In the following sentences, underline the prepositional phrases and circle the words being modified.

1. (People) in the news are frequently embarrassed.
2. The (drugstore) in town is open today.
3. The (musical) with the best choreography will win.
4. A (gorilla) in a red jumpsuit and a (chimpanzee) in a chiffon dress ran into the tent.
5. The (cottage) beside the gurgling brook was sold a year ago.
6. The (list) of students' addresses was burned in the fire this morning.
7. (Nobody) in this class knows.
8. The (doctors) in this hospital are working very hard.
9. The (combination) to the safe is lost.
10. The (CD) on the computer is amazing.

• Write your own sentences using the prepositional phrases below as adjectives. Underline the phrase and circle the preposition.

1. for the defense _Sentences will vary._
2. beside the lake _____
3. below the green umbrella _____
4. above the slimy seaweed _____
5. amid the thick fog _____
6. with the red flag _____
7. on the sailboat _____

Adverb Prepositional Phrases

Like a one-word adverb, an adverb prepositional phrase usually modifies a verb and may tell *where, how,* or *when* an action takes place.
We play ball <u>in the park</u>. (Tells *where* we *play*)
She called <u>in a loud voice</u>. (Tells *how* she *called*)
Mom gave us smiles <u>throughout the day</u>. (Tells *when* Mom *gave*)

• In the following sentences, underline the prepositional phrases and circle the words being modified.

1. The stands (sagged) under the students' weight.
2. My biology book (fell) into the puddle.
3. Ron, the champion runner, (jumped) over the hurdle with ease.
4. The gifts were (wrapped) with care and (placed) under the tree.
5. Marithia and Tinita (walked) under the bridge.
6. Several jumpers (pushed) from the plane too early.
7. The firefighters (rushed) into the forest.
8. After the defeat the team (traveled) alone through the night.
9. You will find Gerald (sitting) behind the barn.
10. The Amish (travel) everywhere in their buggies.
11. The birds (flew) into the tree.
12. The girl (danced) with graceful movements.
13. Lightning (flashes) around the clouds.
14. A tornado (moves) with shocking speed.

• Write your own sentences using the prepositional phrases below as adverbs. Underline the phrase and circle the preposition.

1. in another language _Sentences will vary._
2. in his math class _____
3. under the bed _____
4. during the fifth inning _____

Interjections

> Interjections are words that express strong feeling or sudden emotion. They may be followed by an exclamation point or a comma. Interjections are more effective when they are not overused.
>
> Hey! Look at that hawk. <u>Oh</u>, that's a surprise.

- Underline the interjections in the following sentences.

1. <u>Wow</u>! It's my birthday today!
2. <u>Great</u>! I can't wait for my friends to get here.
3. <u>No</u>! What do you mean they can't come?
4. <u>Oh no</u>! This is terrible!
5. <u>Oh</u>, quit complaining.
6. <u>Rats</u>! I thought this was going to be a great day.
7. <u>Zounds</u>! I have an idea!
8. <u>Shh</u>, listen.
9. <u>Yes</u>! This just might work.
10. <u>Right</u>! I'll call some of my other friends and see if they can come.
11. <u>Ah</u>, I love that idea.
12. <u>Hey</u>! Did you hear that?
13. <u>Surprise</u>! We came after all!
14. <u>Gosh</u>! I sure was worried for a while.
15. <u>Super</u>! It was a great celebration!

- Use the interjections given here to write sentences of your own.

1. Hey _____Sentences will vary._____
2. Wow _____
3. Alas _____
4. Stop _____
5. Ouch _____

- Write two sentences describing a ride at an amusement park. Include an interjection in each sentence.

1. _____Sentences will vary._____
2. _____

Conjunctions

> A conjunction is a word that joins words or groups of words together. There are three types of conjunctions: coordinating, correlative, and subordinating.
> **Coordinating conjunctions:** and, but, or, nor, for, yet, so
> **Correlative conjunctions:** either—or, both—and, whether—or, neither—nor, not only—but also (These are always used in pairs.)
> **Some common subordinating conjunctions:** after, although, as, as if, because, before, if, since, that, though, until, when, while

- In the following sentences, circle the conjunctions. Identify what kind of conjunction each is by writing letters in the blanks: **CO**—coordinating, **CR**—correlative, **SU**—subordinating.

CO 1. Moscow is Russia's largest city (and) its political capital as well.
CO 2. It is also a commercial, cultural, (and) communications center.
CO 3. It is known as a center for heavy machinery manufacturing, (but) it has other important industries.
CR 4. (Neither) the czars (nor) the communist dictators were able to take the heart from Moscow's people.
SU 5. We will understand the people of Moscow (if) we study their history.
SU 6. Some of that history was hidden, (though) it is now coming to light.
SU 7. (Though) Moscow remained an important center of culture and trade, St. Petersburg became the new capital.
SU 8. Moscow was somewhat weakened (because) every effort was made to make St. Petersburg the center of attention.
CO 9. This was encouraged for two centuries (but) was stopped in 1917 with the Russian Revolution.
SU 10. The capital was once again Moscow (when) the government fell to the Bolsheviks.
CO 11. Moscow grew rapidly in the 1930s (and) the city gained power.
CR 12. During World War II, Germans (not only) used planes to bomb the city (but also) approached the city with foot soldiers.

- Write three sentences about your country, using a conjunction in each. Underline the conjunction.

1. _____Sentences will vary._____
2. _____
3. _____

Same Word—Different Part of Speech

> There are many words whose function as a part of speech varies depending on how they are used in a particular sentence.
> The answer was <u>right</u>. (an adjective)
> What <u>right</u> do you have to say that? (a noun)
> I will <u>right</u> all of the wrongs committed. (a verb)

- Identify the part of speech of each boldfaced word: adjective, adverb, noun, pronoun, verb, or preposition.

adverb 1. He slid **down** head first.
noun 2. Did you notice an unusual **smell** when you walked in?
pronoun 3. **Some** are planning to visit the art museum while others are intending to go out for lunch.
noun 4. The people of this **country** want real leadership.
preposition 5. The itsy-bitsy spider slid **down** the water spout.
verb 6. I **smell** a rat!
adjective 7. Doris signed up for a class in **country** painting.
adjective 8. **Some** people really enjoyed the dance we went to last night.
noun 9. Terri said that it was the most moving **play** she had ever seen.
verb 10. Hannah **played** with her little sister while I fixed dinner.

- Write your own sentences using the following words as the specified parts of speech given below.

1. musical (noun) _____Sentences will vary._____
2. safe (adjective) _____
3. work (verb) _____
4. train (noun) _____
5. musical (adjective) _____
6. safe (noun) _____
7. work (noun) _____
8. train (verb) _____

Identifying Parts of Speech—Review

> **Noun**—names a person, place, thing, or idea
> **Pronoun**—takes the place of a noun
> **Verb**—shows action or state of being
> **Adjective**—modifies a noun or pronoun
> **Adverb**—modifies a verb, adjective, or another adverb
> **Preposition**—relates a noun or pronoun to another word
> **Conjunction**—links words or groups of words
> **Interjection**—expresses strong emotion or surprise

- In each of the following sentences, identify the part of speech of the underlined word.

adverb 1. A city must be planned <u>carefully</u>, or people will not want to live in it.
verb 2. We were going to attend the game, but the meteorologist <u>predicted</u> rain.
pronoun 3. I am going to do <u>my</u> homework after school, but I would rather play with my friends.
noun 4. Sheila put a <u>dollar</u> into the pop machine, but nothing came out.
preposition 5. Doris skidded <u>around</u> the corner, and she lost control of the car.
adverb 6. The paperboy drove <u>past</u>, and he threw the paper into the bushes.
conjunction 7. Wash the car <u>and</u> wax it.
pronoun 8. My mother and I went to two movies and liked <u>both</u> of them.
verb 9. How will you <u>pay</u> for this damage, and when can I expect the money?
conjunction 10. Gloria will examine the car, <u>though</u> Ted will buy it.
adjective 11. The catfish swam near <u>the</u> surface, and the cat tried to snag him.
verb 12. The team won the game, and the crowd <u>waited</u> outside the stadium to cheer them.
noun 13. A fee must be paid, or you will not be allowed to use this <u>facility</u>.
adverb 14. Either the test was <u>very</u> difficult, or those students are not studying hard enough.
adjective 15. The Trojan War was made <u>famous</u> in Homer's *Iliad*.
adjective 16. Vancouver is a <u>popular</u> tourist destination.
noun 17. The Biblical name for <u>Israel</u> and surrounding land was Canaan.
noun 18. The Arthurian legends tell the <u>tale</u> of King Arthur and his Knights of the Round Table.
preposition 19. The Battle of Manila Bay was fought <u>during</u> the Spanish-American War.
interjection 20. <u>Wow</u>! Trent is going to visit the new museum.

Participles and Participial Phrases

A participle is a verb form that functions as an adjective. A participial phrase is a group of words that includes the participle and its related words.

The present participle is usually formed by adding -ing to the present tense verb.
Participle: The runner enjoyed the cooling breezes.
Participial phrase: Cooling off, the runners jumped into the pool.

The past participle is usually formed by adding -ed to the present tense. Check your dictionary for the way irregular verbs form the past participle.
Participle: Each sunburned person would be uncomfortable tonight.
Participial phrase: Burned by the sun, the teenager reached for a t-shirt.

• In each of the following sentences, underline the participle and circle the word that it modifies.

1. We tiptoed around the sleeping child.
2. The surging river terrified the townspeople.
3. Each contestant auditioned her singing voice for the pageant.
4. The dried flowers were carefully hung in the barn.
5. The satisfied customers left the restaurant determined to come back.
6. The city removed the wrecked cars.
7. A watched pot never boils.
8. You could tell he was scared because of his shaking knees.
9. A startling rumor spread quickly through the school.
10. Jane owns a flourishing business.

• In each of the following sentences, underline the participial phrase and circle the word that it modifies.

1. Opening the door, Greg saw a huge crowd of people.
2. The car pictured in the brochure was a Chevy.
3. Donald saw a giraffe eating leaves.
4. Breathing hard, the runner collapsed.
5. The police, knocking loudly on the door, awakened everybody.
6. Entering the store, Frieda walked down the center aisle.
7. Slipping into the water, the diver disappeared.
8. Walking quickly, Ron soon reached the depot.

Page 84

Gerunds and Gerund Phrases

A gerund is a verb form ending in -ing that functions as a noun. Gerunds are formed by adding -ing to the present tense verb form.
Painting is my favorite hobby.
A gerund phrase is a group of words that includes a gerund and its related words.
Painting the ceiling is a difficult job.

• In each of the following sentences, underline the gerund and indicate how it is being used in the sentence: subject (S,) direct object (DO), object of preposition (OP), or predicate noun (PN).

S   1. Exercising is the best thing you can do for yourself.
PN   2. My favorite hobby is skiing.
DO   3. Don enjoys painting.
DO   4. Sarah likes skating.
S   5. The tolling of the bells is getting on my nerves.
S   6. Whispering is not polite.
OP   7. You can become a pro by practicing.
S   8. Jogging has become a very popular activity.
DO   9. Whenever I go to a swim meet, I enjoy the diving most.

• In the following sentences, underline the gerund phrase and indicate its use in the sentence (S, DO, OP, PN).

OP   1. Susan was soon bored with reading her book.
DO   2. Teresa enjoys reading historical novels.
S   3. Flipping hamburgers is a good way to make some money.
OP   4. The referee began by introducing the players to one another.
S   5. Drinking a lot of water is good for you.
PN   6. Ron's new task is collecting newspapers to recycle.
S   7. Asking questions is probably the best way to learn something.
S   8. Playing baseball is my idea of an enjoyable afternoon.
S   9. Measuring the ingredients in the recipe will ensure good results.
OP 10. She passed her opponent by running faster.
PN 11. His goal was playing chess in the world championship.

Page 85

Infinitives and Infinitive Phrases

An infinitive is a present tense verb and is usually preceded by to. It is often used as a noun serving as a subject, a direct object, or a predicate noun.
To win the race is her goal. (subject)
She hopes to win. (direct object)
Ellen's goal is to win the race. (predicate noun)

• In each of the following sentences, underline the infinitive. Indicate if the infinitive is used as a subject (S), a direct object (DO), or predicate noun (PN).

DO   1. On a snowy day I like to ski.
S   2. To fish is all my grandpa ever wanted out of life.
DO   3. My father was hoping to play.
DO   4. Would you like to go?
S   5. To debate is the reason that we are gathered here.
S   6. To sleep was my only thought.
PN   7. One sacred responsibility is to vote.
DO   8. I did not dare to speak.
PN   9. The purpose of talking is to communicate.

• In each of the following sentences, underline the infinitive phrase which is used as a noun and indicate whether it is a subject (S), a direct object (DO), or predicate noun (PN).

PN   1. The club's goal was to raise one thousand dollars.
DO   2. Gilda expected to pass the class with ease.
DO   3. Seth decided to go to the game by himself.
S   4. To finish this paper by tomorrow will be very difficult.
DO   5. He did not dare to make the trip alone.
S   6. To win a championship must be very exciting.
DO   7. Several people helped to rescue the boy.
DO   8. The teacher tried to show us several ways of solving the problem.
DO   9. Dorothy wanted to have it all.
S   10. To swing from a rope over the river can be challenging.
DO 11. Those books need to be saved.
DO 12. Chris planned to run for president of his class.
DO 13. The hungry workers hoped to get a good meal.

Page 86

More Verbals

Verbals—participles, gerunds, and infinitives—are verb forms that do not perform as verbs. Instead, they function as other parts of speech.

• In each of the following sentences, underline the verbal phrase and indicate whether it is a participial phrase (P), a gerund phrase (G), or an infinitive phrase (I).

I   1. He was asked to buy some fresh vegetables.
P   2. Known as one of the best pitchers in baseball, Warren Spahn was inducted into the Hall of Fame.
G   3. Kelly practices juggling three apples at a time.
I   4. Lexi tried to study on a regular basis.
I   5. It is important to exercise every day.
P   6. Talking to himself, my brother walked down the street.
I   7. Reggie volunteered to have everybody over for dinner.
G   8. Taking a vitamin is the way he starts his day.
P   9. Standing up to his knees in the water, Wes cast his fly into the river.
I   10. The boys all want to go to the amusement park.
P   11. Exhausted from the long journey, the fish wallowed in the shallow water.
G   12. Hooking rugs is a very interesting hobby for many.
P   13. The principal, depressed by the poor attendance, worked on a new plan.
G   14. Baking cookies helps relieve my tension.
G   15. Anne likes painting seashells.

• Write your own sentences including the indicated verb forms.

1. (participial)   Sentences will vary.
2. (participial)
3. (gerund)
4. (gerund)
5. (infinitive)
6. (infinitive)

Page 87

IF8732 Grammar 7–8

Misplaced and Dangling Modifiers

> Modifiers that are not placed near the words or phrases that they modify are called misplaced modifiers.
> Misplaced modifier: <u>Chilled to the bone</u>, the hot soup tasted good to the skiers.
> (Here *chilled to the bone* modifies the word *skiers* but is not placed near it.)

• Underline the misplaced modifiers and then write the sentences correctly.

1. The women's group is offering counseling for those who need it <u>on Monday</u>.

   The women's group is offering counseling on Monday for....

2. The new car was very popular with the race fans <u>which raced past</u>.

   The new car, which raced past, was very popular....

3. The company decided to buy a new building <u>which needed more space</u>.

   The company, which needed more space, decided to buy....

4. The number increases every year <u>of boating accidents</u>.

   The number of boating accidents increases every year.

5. There is a special item in that store <u>that is on sale today</u>.

   There is a special item that is on sale today in that store.

> If a modifying word, phrase, or clause does not modify a particular word, then the modifier is called a dangling modifier. Every modifier must have a word that it clearly modifies.
> Incorrect: <u>Entering the bay</u>, the city loomed in front of us.
> (*Entering the bay* does not modify *city*)
> Correct: <u>Entering the bay</u>, the boat began to head toward shore.
> (*Entering the bay* correctly modifies *the boat*)

• In the following sentences, underline the dangling modifiers. If the modifier is used correctly, write **OK** in the blank.

_____ 1. <u>Chilled by the snow</u>, it felt good to be inside.

OK 2. In the summer catalog, the models looked elegant.

_____ 3. <u>Living on the beach all summer</u>, the sun-block supply was quite low.

_____ 4. <u>Startled by the wild animal</u>, the scream caused me to whirl around suddenly.

OK 5. Living in the woods, the trapper was a contented man.

_____ 6. <u>Humbled by the speech</u>, the look that was given said it all.

OK 7. After it had been scraped, the toast tasted fine.

Independent and Dependent Clauses

> An independent clause is a group of words with a subject and a predicate that expresses a complete thought and can stand by itself as a sentence.
> <u>Jack played golf</u> until it was too dark to see.
> (Independent clause)
>
> A dependent clause cannot stand alone. It depends upon the independent clause of the sentence to complete its meaning. Dependent clauses start with words like *who, which, that, because, when, if, until, before,* and *after.*
> <u>If the people support Hank</u>, he will run.
> (Dependent clause)

• In each of the following sentences, underline the independent clause once and the dependent clause twice.

1. <u>When the cold weather arrives</u>, <u>I'm going south</u>.

2. <u>The whole class really enjoyed the movie</u> <u>that showed life under the sea</u>.

3. <u>If you think you know the answer</u>, <u>raise your hand</u>.

4. <u>I was about to leave for my vacation</u> <u>when I noticed that the tire was flat</u>.

5. <u>Fred really liked the car</u> <u>that we bought for him at the auction</u>.

6. <u>Theresa was really disappointed</u> <u>that we could not go</u>.

7. <u>Until history became Henry's favorite subject</u>, <u>it was not easy for him to get a good grade</u>.

8. <u>When David builds a new radio-controlled car</u>, <u>we're going to race each other</u>.

9. <u>The cottage</u> <u>which we had purchased</u> <u>was old and dilapidated</u>.

10. <u>If the pain does not go away</u>, <u>please call the doctor</u>.

11. <u>Sheila knows many people</u> <u>who can play bridge</u>.

12. <u>Ted thought he knew just how she felt</u> <u>because he'd had the same experience</u>.

13. <u>I have not yet heard the song</u> <u>that the popular singer recorded in Finnish</u>.

14. <u>The paramedics grabbed the oxygen</u> <u>when they saw the patient turning blue</u>.

15. <u>You have not lived</u> <u>until you take a trip down the Colorado River in a raft</u>.

16. <u>When I returned to the store</u>, <u>he had already left</u>.

17. <u>She wants a new truck</u> <u>that will handle well on rough terrain</u>.

Adjective Clauses

> An adjective clause is a dependent clause that functions as an adjective. It can modify any noun or pronoun in a sentence.
> The politician <u>who won the election</u> saluted his supporters.

• In each of the following sentences, underline the adjective clause and circle the word it modifies.

1. Shawn knows the (teacher) <u>who gave you the detention</u>.

2. (Traditions) <u>that seem to have disappeared</u> often return.

3. The painter tried to match the (color) <u>that was used before</u>.

4. The (activity) <u>that Gentry most enjoyed</u> was diving from the falls.

5. I bought the (desk) <u>that was in the front window</u>.

6. He put his hand under the (table) <u>that had been freshly painted</u>.

7. Sally is the (person) <u>who applied for the job</u>.

8. The police (officer) <u>whose gun fell from his holster</u> was very embarrassed.

9. The (lake) <u>where they caught all of the fish</u> was far away.

10. The (city) <u>which we visited</u> was one of the cleanest in the state.

11. The (play) <u>to which the critic referred</u> was a bomb.

12. The (horse) <u>that I bet on</u> fell during the race.

13. You will have to tell me the names of the (students) <u>who might help us</u>.

14. A (wall) <u>that faces south</u> will absorb a lot of solar heat.

• Write five sentences about your neighborhood. Include an adjective clause in each. Underline each adjective clause and circle the noun or pronoun modified.

1. *Sentences will vary.*
2. _____
3. _____
4. _____
5. _____

Adverb Clauses

> An adverb clause is a dependent clause that functions as an adverb. It can modify a verb, an adjective, or another adverb. Adverb clauses tell *how, when, where,* or *why* an action happened.
> We ate <u>when Grandpa arrived</u>. (modifies *ate*; tells *when*)

• In each of the following sentences, underline the adverb clause and write the question it answers: **how, when, where,** or **why**.

when 1. You should listen carefully <u>when the teacher speaks</u>.

why 2. <u>Since I read the book</u>, I disliked the movie.

when 3. The doctor was very nervous <u>before he began the surgery</u>.

when 4. Everything began <u>when Jed entered the room</u>.

why 5. Ellen's reading will be the last <u>because it is the best</u>.

why 6. <u>Because you have been so nice</u>, I will allow you to move ahead of me.

when 7. <u>Before Julie started running</u>, she felt tired all the time.

where 8. He looked <u>where the backpack was last seen</u>.

how 9. I can stay afloat <u>by moving my arms</u>.

when 10. <u>After the class is over</u>, I will tell you a secret about the professor.

when 11. <u>When you get to the light</u>, turn left.

why 12. She practiced every day <u>because she wanted to join the team</u>.

why 13. <u>Since the book was about Hawaii</u>, I found it interesting.

when 14. Ken visited his mother <u>whenever he could</u>.

when 15. <u>Before the practice began</u>, the coach gave a short pep talk.

• Write five sentences about a hobby you enjoy. For each sentence, include an adverb clause which answers the indicated question.

1. (how)   *Sentences will vary.*
2. (when) _____
3. (where) _____
4. (why) _____

© Carson-Dellosa   125   IF8732 Grammar 7–8

Noun Clauses

A noun clause is a dependent clause that functions as a noun. It may be used as a subject, a direct object, an indirect object, an object of a preposition, or a predicate noun.
  <u>What happened</u> surprised everyone. (subject)
  George wondered <u>what he could do</u>. (direct object)
  Alyson will give <u>whoever wants one</u> a cookie. (indirect object)
  The children did not laugh until <u>the end of the play</u>. (object of preposition)
  The problem is <u>what we will eat when we get there</u>. (predicate noun)

- In each of the following sentences, underline the noun clause and indicate how the clause is used in the sentence—subject (**S**), direct object (**DO**), indirect object (**IO**), object of a preposition (**OP**), or predicate noun (**PN**).

S 1. <u>That you should eat your vegetables</u> is certainly true.

S 2. <u>What Heather did today</u> was very difficult.

DO 3. The meteorologists agreed <u>that rain was expected</u>.

OP 4. The bus will depart at <u>whatever time you designate</u>.

PN 5. A good movie is <u>what I would like to see today</u>.

IO 6. I will give <u>whoever comes to the door</u> the message.

S 7. <u>Whose books these are</u> is obvious.

OP 8. This prize will be awarded to <u>whoever completes the course</u>.

PN 9. Life is <u>what you make it</u>.

S 10. <u>What you say</u> is not the truth.

S 11. <u>How a computer works</u> is a mystery to me.

S 12. <u>Whoever wrote this graffiti</u> will be punished.

PN 13. A chance at the big time was <u>what the minor league players craved</u>.

DO 14. I know <u>that this plan will work</u>.

- Write five sentences of your own, each of which includes a noun clause used as indicated.
  1. (direct object) _Sentences will vary._
  2. (subject) _____
  3. (predicate noun) _____
  4. (object of a preposition) _____
  5. (indirect object) _____

Identifying Clauses

An adjective clause is a dependent clause that functions as an adjective modifying nouns or pronouns.
An adverb clause is a dependent clause that functions as an adverb modifying verbs, adjectives, or other adverbs.
A noun clause is a dependent clause that functions as a noun.

- In each of the following sentences, underline the dependent clause and indicate if it is an adjective clause (**ADJ**), an adverb clause (**ADV**), or a noun clause (**N**).

N 1. Davis read the pamphlet to <u>whoever would listen</u>.

N 2. <u>How you play the game</u> is important.

ADJ 3. Green is a color <u>that is considered soothing</u>.

ADV 4. I would like you to wait <u>so that we can go together</u>.

N 5. We already know <u>what his real problem is</u>.

ADJ 6. The tornado <u>that hit the town</u> destroyed many homes.

ADV 7. Greg eats hotdogs <u>when he is at the ball park</u>.

ADV 8. Ralph played <u>until he could barely move</u>.

N 9. The director denied <u>that he had stolen the idea for the movie</u>.

ADJ 10. Lake Superior, <u>which is one of the Great Lakes</u>, is the largest of the five.

N 11. The really bad news was <u>that we couldn't go to the play</u>.

ADJ 12. The painting <u>that we lost</u> is worth a lot of money.

ADV 13. <u>When the fish jumped out of the water</u>, we realized that it was huge.

- Add an independent clause to each of the dependent clauses below to make a complete sentence.
  1. **who fell from the tree** (adjective clause) _Sentences will vary._
  2. **that her dress was beautiful** (noun clause) _____
  3. **when the river rises above this point** (adverb clause) _____

Punctuating Direct Quotations

Quotation marks are used to enclose direct quotations. The end punctuation usually comes before the final quotation mark at the end of the quote.
  Mary said, "Where are we going?"
Always capitalize the first word of a direct quotation. Do not capitalize the first word in the second part of an interrupted quote unless the second part begins a new sentence.
  "When it starts to snow," he said, "put on your heavy coat."
  "Where did he go?" asked Bob. "We need him."

- Correctly punctuate and add capitals to the following sentences.
  1. look out cried Jackie
     "Look out!" cried Jackie.
  2. didn't you see that broken step Jackie asked
     "Didn't you see that broken step?" Jackie asked.
  3. no said Anne thanks for warning me
     "No," said Anne. "Thanks for warning me."
  4. i think we should fix that before someone gets hurt Jackie suggested
     "I think we should fix that before someone gets hurt," Jackie suggested.
  5. do you know where there's a hammer Ann queried
     "Do you know where there's a hammer?" Ann queried.
  6. i don't admitted Jackie but maybe Emily does
     "I don't," admitted Jackie, "but maybe Emily does."
  7. hey Emily she yelled where's the hammer
     "Hey, Emily!" she yelled. "Where's the hammer?"
  8. don't yell responded Emily i'm right behind you
     "Don't yell," responded Emily. "I'm right behind you."

- Write three sentences with direct quotations below. Include at least one interrogative and one exclamatory quotation.
  1. _Sentences will vary._
  2. _____
  3. _____

Direct/Indirect Quotations

A direct quotation is the use of someone's exact words. It is always set off with quotation marks.
  Kati said, "I am going to the beach today."
An indirect quotation is the writer's description of someone else's words. It does not require quotation marks.
  Dave said that Kati was going to the beach today.

- For each of the following sentences, write **DQ** (direct quotation) or **IQ** (indirect quotation) in the blank. Then add quotation marks wherever they are needed.

DQ 1. Phoebe said, "We're going to the Winter Olympics!"

DQ 2. "How are you getting there?" asked Jaime.

IQ 3. At the same time, Della asked Phoebe what her favorite event was.

DQ 4. "We're flying," said Phoebe, "and I can't wait to go!"

IQ 5. Jeff said that he'd never flown in an airplane.

IQ 6. Phoebe then said her favorite event is figure skating.

DQ 7. "Are you really going to see the figure skating?" asked Anne.

DQ 8. Phoebe said, "Yes, my father has already bought tickets."

DQ 9. "Well, I'd rather see the downhill skiing," interjected Jaime.

IQ 10. Anne said that she would rather see something beautiful and not have to worry about people getting hurt.

IQ 11. Della said she understood what Anne was talking about.

DQ 12. "May I come along with you?" implored Della.

- Write two sentences that contain direct quotations and two sentences that contain indirect quotations.
  1. (direct) _Sentences will vary._
  2. (direct) _____
  3. (indirect) _____
  4. (indirect) _____

Other Uses for Quotation Marks

> **Single quotation marks are used to set off a quotation within a quotation.**
> "When did you tell me, 'I'm going with you'?" asked Dad.
> The commercial asked, "How do you spell 'relief'?"
> **Quotation marks are used to set off words, phrases, or sentences referred to within a sentence.**
> You spell relief "r-e-l-i-e-f."
> **Quotation marks are used to set off slang words and expressions.**
> The pitcher threw the hitter a "spitter."
> **Quotation marks are used to set off the titles of magazine articles, names of songs, titles of poems, and chapters of books.**
> The magazine always includes a section entitled "Letters to the Editor."

• Add quotation marks as needed to the sentences below.

1. "Chicago" is my favorite poem," said Bill.

2. "That's just because you grew up there," replied Rickie.

3. "That's not true," corrected Bill. "I like the way Sandburg writes."

4. "When Bill said, 'I like the way Sandburg writes,' I think he really meant it," added Hillary.

5. "Did you do your homework yet?" asked Bob.

6. "I read the chapter 'Westward Bound' in my history book," said Georgia.

7. Georgia started singing "Home on the Range."

8. The class read "The Gift of the Magi."

9. Sara wondered if "The Furnished Room" was included in that book of short stories.

10. The term "short story" is defined in the glossary.

11. George wondered what authors the teacher considered "flaky."

12. "What kind of question is that?" the teacher asked.

13. "Is that word in the dictionary?" inquired Alex.

14. "Did George say, 'I'll look that up'? inquired the teacher.

Comma Use

> **A comma is used to set off an introductory phrase or a dependent clause.**
> When you get home, we'll go to the mall.
> **A comma is used after words of direct address at the beginning of the sentence.**
> Michael, call me when you get home.
> **A comma is used after introductory words such as *yes, indeed, well, in addition, thus,* and *moreover.***
> Yes, I agree with you completely.
> Thus, the game ended before it had begun.
> **Use two commas to set off interrupting words or expressions.**
> Have you, by the way, ordered lunch yet?

• Add commas to the following sentences.

1. When I graduate from high school, I plan to go to college.

2. Yes, that is a good idea.

3. Of course, you will need good grades to get into the college of your choice.

4. Seeing that you are a good student, I know you'll have no problem.

5. In addition, your involvement in extracurricular activities is important.

6. Ted, what will you be studying in college?

7. If I get there, I'd like to study oceanography.

8. Well, you will have your work cut out for you.

9. You will find, I'm sure, that it is a competitive field.

10. Indeed, it won't be easy.

11. Jack, how about you?

12. I would like, I think, to go to medical school.

13. Fortunately, I've been studying hard all year.

• Write three sentences, each having a correctly punctuated introductory element.

1. _____ *Sentences will vary.* _____
2. _____
3. _____

Capitalization

> **The words *north, south, east,* and *west* are not capitalized when they refer to directions. They are capitalized when they refer to specific sections of the country.**
> Henry traveled *east* to see his sister.
> Henry traveled to the *East Coast* to see his mother.
> **The names given to planets and stars are capitalized, but the words like planet, sun, moon, and star are not capitalized.**
> The pieces of the comet bombarded *Jupiter.*
> The *moon* rose in the night sky.
> **The words derived from proper nouns are usually capitalized.**
> The *American* tourists started snapping pictures.
> **Names of deities and sacred books are capitalized.**
> *Jehovah,* the *Koran*

• In each of the following sentences, circle the words that should be capitalized.

1. (we) live east of the river.

2. (living) in the (midwest) gives one a different view of the world.

3. (the) two scientists disagreed about the impact of the comet.

4. (if) you drive far enough north, you will avoid the traffic jams.

5. (yolanda) likes to watch the (latin american) dances.

7. (some) people had a hard time realizing that the (south) had lost the war.

8. (there) is a passage in the (bible) which talks about forgiveness.

9. (the) boy studied the (talmud.)

• Use the words below to write sentences of your own which are correctly punctuated and capitalized.

1. german _____ *Sentences will vary.* _____

2. elizabethan theater _____

3. venus _____

4. the mideast _____

5. the south _____

More Capitalization

> **Capitalize special titles when they precede a person's name.**
> You would never guess that Doctor Gregory is a brain surgeon.
> **Capitalize geographic names.**
> Our family made the drive up Pikes Peak.
> **Capitalize the names of streets, bridges, dams, hotels, monuments, parks, etc.**
> My brother was in a demonstration in Grant Park.
> **Capitalize the names of historical periods, historical events, and historical documents.**
> We just finished studying the French Revolution.
> **Capitalize the names of government bodies and departments.**
> The Food and Drug Administration approved the new serum for public use.

• Circle the words that need capitals.

1. Have you ever sailed on (lake) (michigan?)

2. The (battle) of (midway) was a turning point in (world) (war) II.

3. The bill sponsored by (senator) (javits) was defeated.

4. The (plaza) (hotel) in (new) (york) (city) is one of the most famous hotels in the world.

5. He was elected to the (house) of (representatives.)

6. The senators walked toward the (white) (house.)

7. Maybe we could get that information from the (library) of (congress.)

• Use the words below to write sentences of your own which are correctly punctuated and capitalized.

1. president washington _____ *Sentences will vary.* _____

2. the u.s. postal service _____

3. san francisco bay _____

4. the battle of gettysburg _____

And More Capitalization

Capitalize the main words in the titles of books, movies, magazines, songs, etc. Do not capitalize prepositions, coordinate conjunctions, or articles unless they are the first or last words of the title.

Pride and Prejudice is my favorite book.

Do not capitalize the names of school subjects unless they are languages or unless they are followed by a number indicating a specific course.

Wally is taking English and biology this term.

All freshmen must take Algebra 101.

Capitalize words that show family relationship when they are used instead of a name or as part of a name.

My Uncle Don has the greatest sense of humor.

Does your uncle have a sense of humor?

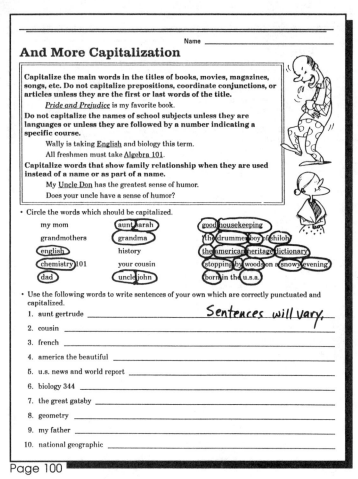

• Circle the words which should be capitalized.

my mom	aunt sarah	good housekeeping
grandmothers	grandma	the drummer boy of shiloh
english	history	the american heritage dictionary
chemistry 101	your cousin	stopping by woods on a snowy evening
dad	uncle john	born in the u.s.a.

• Use the following words to write sentences of your own which are correctly punctuated and capitalized.

Sentences will vary.

1. aunt gertrude _____
2. cousin _____
3. french _____
4. america the beautiful _____
5. u.s. news and world report _____
6. biology 344 _____
7. the great gatsby _____
8. geometry _____
9. my father _____
10. national geographic _____

Problem Pairs

There are certain pairs of words which are frequently confused; some sound alike, some are spelled similarly, and some have similar meanings.

already – previously; **all ready** – all prepared
altogether – entirely; **all together** – everyone in one group or place
its – possessive form of it; **it's** – contraction of "it is"
there – at that place; **their** – possessive form of they; **they're** – contraction of "they are"
than – conjunction used in comparisons; **then** – at that time
who's – contraction of "who is" or "who has"; **whose** – possessive form of who

• Circle the correct word choice in the following sentences.

1. (Whose, Who's) party did you attend?
2. We had (all ready, already) made the turn when we realized our mistake.
3. A reunion is a great time to get everyone (all together, altogether).
4. Leave that package (their, there) where you found it.
5. My team is much better (than, then) yours.
6. (Its, It's) just the way he plays the game.
7. (Whose, Who's) that student at the end of the hall?
8. We were (all ready, already) to go when we saw the flat tire.
9. We were not (all together, altogether) pleased with that book.
10. (Their, There) luggage was lost somewhere in the terminal.
11. If I pay for the tickets, (then, than) will you go?
12. (Their, They're) going to the baseball game.
13. (Its, It's) still raining.
14. The dog did not like (its, it's) collar.
15. I (already, all ready) have a dog.
16. I like tomato soup better (then, than) chicken noodle soup.
17. (Who's, Whose) jacket is this?
18. The football is over (there, their).

More Problem Pairs

Certain pairs of words are often confused. The best defense against making a mistake with these words is to consult a dictionary.

brake – a mechanism for slowing down or stopping; **break** – to shatter or come apart
later – more late; **latter** – the second of two persons or things mentioned
lead – to go first, or a heavy metal; **led** – past tense of "lead"
loose – free, not tight; **lose** – to suffer the loss of
principal – head of a school, or important; **principle** – a rule of conduct, or a basic truth
plane – a flat surface, or an airplane; **plain** – not fancy, or a large area of flat land

• Circle the correct word choice in the following sentences.

1. The student driver missed the (break, brake) with his foot.
2. We will be going (later, latter) than you.
3. The room was lined with (led, lead) to protect the technician from the x-rays.
4. I went to the dentist because my tooth was (lose, loose).
5. The (principal, principle) works hard for her school.
6. She (led, lead) the way in the field of chemical engineering.
7. You don't have anything to (lose, loose).
8. I believe it is important to understand the (principle, principal) of gravity.
9. The glass will (break, brake) if you bump into it.
10. Henry thought that the (later, latter) of the two reasons made more sense.
11. The (plane, plain) was forced to make an emergency landing.
12. My tastes run to very (plain, plane) designs.
13. I will tell you about my problem (later, latter).
14. Follow these (principles, principals), and you will be a success.
15. The science students rolled the marble down the inclined (plain, plane).
16. We don't want the tigers to (loose, lose) their freedom.
17. The inspectors checked for traces of (lead, led) in the water.
18. The helicopter landed easily on the (plane, plain).

About the Author

Mark Dressel received both his bachelor's and master's degrees in the Teaching of Reading from Western Michigan University. He has taught remedial reading and Advanced Placement English for over twenty years at the high school level. Mark currently teaches humanities and serves as a consultant for several school districts on writing across the curriculum projects.

Credits

Author: Mark Dressel
Artist: Catherine Yuh
Cover Photo: Frank Pieroni
Project Director/Editor: Rhonda DeWaard
Editors: Sharon Kirkwood, Lisa Hancock
Production: Pat Geasler